**The Creatures
Time Forgot**

David Hevey was born in 1959, the sixth of seven children in an Irish, working-class family in Southend-on-Sea, Essex. He became an epileptic at the age of sixteen. After completing a course in Fine Art Painting at Brighton Polytechnic, he did a variety of jobs, including working as a grill chef and as a seafront photographer, which he combined with political activism and fine art painting.

David Hevey began his photographic career as a photo-journalist working for publications such as the Times Educational Supplement, New Statesman and New Society. The fusion in his photographic practice of his fine art training, his experience as a seafront photographer and his epileptic hallucinations led to his decision to become an issue-based photographer working with disability representation. His clients have included the Trades Union movement, local authorities, the United Nations and the disability movement. His work has been featured in four major exhibitions: A Sense of Self and Striking Poses (1988); Beyond the Barriers: Disability, Sexuality and Personal Relationships (1990) and Access to Image: Photographs by David Hevey, a one-person exhibition at the National Museum of Film and Photography, Bradford (1991).

The Creatures Time Forgot forms part of a multi-event project in which David Hevey investigates the process of disability imagery making; it includes a touring exhibition, a training pack and a poster series.

The Creatures Time Forgot

PHOTOGRAPHY AND DISABILITY IMAGERY

by DAVID HEVEY

Additional text and photographs by
JO SPENCE and
JESSICA EVANS

Foreword by
DAWN LANGLEY,
Camerawork Gallery, London

Routledge
LONDON AND NEW YORK

First published 1992
by Routledge
11 New Fetter Lane
London EC4P 4EE

Simultaneously published in the USA and Canada by Routledge
a division of Routledge, Chapman and Hall, INC.
29 West 35th Street, New York, NY 10001

Printed and bound in Great Britain by
Butler and Tanner Ltd, Frome and London

British Library Cataloguing-in-Publication Data
Hevey, David
   The creatures time forgot: photography and disability imagery.
   I. Title   II. Spence, Jo
   779.2

Library of Congress Cataloging-in-Publication Data
Hevey, David
   The creatures time forgot: photography and disability imagery /
   by David Hevey: additional text and photographs by Jo Spence
   and Jessica Evans: foreword by Dawn Langley.
   p.   cm.–(Pack and a poster series)
   1. Handicapped–Great Britain–Pictorial works.   2. Photography.
   Artistic.   I. Title.   II. Series.
   HV1559.G6H48   1992
   362.4'092–dc20   91-36459

ISBN 0-415-07019-8

∞ Printed on permanent paper manufactured in accordance with
American NISO Standards

O wad some Pow'r the giftie gie us
To see oursels as others see us!
ROBERT BURNS

To my mother and father,
Kathleen and Christy Hevey,
and to my sisters and brothers.

And to Helena.

And finally, to the disability movement.

Venceremos!

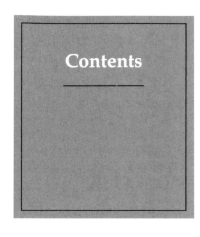

Contents

List of plates

(Apart from charity posters, all images
are by David Hevey unless stated
otherwise.)

Foreword

Issues of visual representation have been floating around like redundant satellites for several years now, but recently many of the debates have started to converge on the photographic representation of disability and disabled people. However, although much discussion has taken place, there has been very little physical evidence of intervention by disabled people within the current forms of photographic practice.

Camerawork addressed the photographic representation of disability by commissioning new work that dealt specifically with this question. A Sense of Self and Beyond the Barriers were the resulting exhibitions, making real the testimonies of numerous disabled people, and locating them clearly within a public context. As an organisational ally to the disability movement, the crucial aspect of these projects lay in consolidating the public profile needed to make the opinions of disabled people heard.

Other actions were taking place in parallel; some worthy, some not so worthy. The King's Fund Centre held a conference entitled 'They Are Not in the Brief', and while the foundation on which the conference was built may be questioned, it undoubtedly served to unite allies within the disability movement and beyond (if only in opposition to some issues of the day). Initially, an ad hoc group consisting of myself (representing Camerawork), David Hevey and Elspeth Morrison (the editor of *Disability Arts in London*) was formed and subsequently a larger committee emerged, including representation from the British Council of Organisations of Disabled People and other disabled-controlled groups.

The purpose of such a grouping was to begin to challenge the negation that is occurring – 'They Are Not in the Brief', for example, appeared to be more concerned with salvaging non-disabled image-making (mainly constructed by the disability charities and their ad agencies) than with dealing with self-image-making by disabled people.

Our initial struggle was to prevent the negative ramifications that 'They Are Not in the Brief' and similar events would cause. Accordingly, written demands (see Chapter 7) were distributed to all delegates of the conference – for it was seen to be ominous that we had not been requested to put forward a collective voice for the event.

Camerawork's role within this process was twofold: becoming both supporter and synthesiser. Out of this arose two consequences: first, the growth, through ongoing financial and moral investment, of new models of disabled-controlled photographic practice and, second, the staging of the 'Cap in Hand' conference, a day organised by and for disabled people.

Camerawork had previously hosted the 'Representing Disability' conference that had led to the exhibition A Sense of Self, and thus helped to speed up the shifting of power away from the all-pervading institutions towards disabled people themselves. It is from this laboratory that this book emerged. Camerawork, as an ally of the disability movement, therefore became both activator and reactor within the process that is now evolving.

As an ally to the movement, at a time of potentially major changes in access and representation, we carefully considered our position in the light of other abuses of power that have taken place. We have actively maintained a minority yet proactive role. As discussions developed we offered whatever services we could to maintain the profile of disability imagery within a public environment.

As an individual, concerned with administering the development of Camerawork's disability programme, I felt that a non-passive position was vital. I have witnessed, as a working-class woman, the physical presence of disablement in my family and my class – disablement which meant the loss of work. The issues of denial, negation and powerlessness are therefore central to me, and to the purpose of Camerawork.

Camerawork is like a good Irish stew. A rich blend of photographic practices and concerns. This has allowed us to take an irreverent approach to our programming and to blur the edges between art, documentary, community practices, photojournalism and advertising techniques. The overall strategy of the organisation has been to create social change, using photography in a directly interventionist approach. This would be difficult to achieve through an adherence to one dominant form or practice.

It is from this experimental base that all our projects exploring the photographic representation of disability have emerged. These projects have been a deliberate attempt to break the stylistic conventions of existing mainstream disability charities.

This was not an easy aim to follow, and it has thrown up numerous issues. How do you start a process whereby people can begin to determine their own self-image, and how do you translate this into photographic images? How do you commission people, who have been traditionally excluded from photographic facilities, to produce sometimes very private, possibly self-exposing works for a public forum? If there are no bench-marks or points of comparison, how do you know if you have got it right? How do you prevent the project from being seen as tokenistic, 'jumping on the disabilities bandwagon', or as another attempt by paternalistic charities to pacify and patronise? We did it by raising reasonable amounts of money, doing a lot of talking and holding numerous meetings. We staged conferences to encourage other people to talk about it – only to find, to our horror, that nobody really knew what a positive or alternative representation was!

This concern of feedback, dialogue and results has underpinned the success of the disability programme at Camerawork. Camerawork has provided structured, directed and critical, but essentially unconditional, support. We accepted from the beginning that this was an experimental area, so while we are publicly accountable, we could not be too prescriptive. Fortunately, those who provided financial support also had faith that this formula would work. The vital element, of course, was the existence and growth of the issue of representation within the disability movement.

Even once the projects were completed, the work up and the publications produced, the problems were not over. We then had to consider a more holistic view of the context which our work was entering – we were in danger of letting others off the hook. While the exhibitions which we have fostered are always toured to other venues, it is important that the booking of Camerawork exhibitions is not substituted for the lack of a disability imagery policy within the tour venues. A monthly booking of alternative disability imagery is important, but it is no answer to demands for equal opportunities.

So what is the relationship between our work, disability arts and equal opportunities? These areas interface on different levels, and much of the take-up of our work has been instigated by equal opportunities policies. So, in order to clarify this point, I consulted Camerawork's equal opportunities policy. On obtaining the large policy document, I realised I had left the main office and entered the inner sanctum of the small quiet office at the back. Why was such a vital document filed away in isolation? Were we not supposed to know this document backwards? Were we fulfilling our equal opportunities responsibilities with this document not sovereign?

The failing, I would argue, is with the policies, not the implementation. They encourage organisations and people to follow the letter, not the spirit, of the law. The extensive policy clauses were lifeless, with little capacity to revive themselves. I am sure that many similar organisations, on discovering the difficulty of following such codes, also file them away hoping not to be reminded of them.

At Camerawork we took risks and decided to experiment: we aimed to translate the spirit of the policy into a visual format that could be more easily understood. We also considered the power aspect of these policies and decided that, if this work was to have any meaning, we should talk to the people most affected by the issue. Nothing too radical in that, you might think. But, on meeting with charities, ad agencies, arts organisations and disabled people, it became all too apparent that nobody else, outside of the disability movement, was pursuing the same course of actions.

This book is an important testimony to the struggle to continue radical disability representation. That representation is not a luxury; it is an integral part of a process concerned with access, empowerment, collective action and rights. It is a political agenda. I am not advocating that we all go out and burn our equal opportunities documents. Even buried in filing cabinets they serve as a reminder that there *are* things to be done and that we must all take responsibility for change. My background has taught me that things do not come easily – especially when the rights of some challenge the power of others. What you gain from experience equates with what you commit to it.

This is Camerawork's observation. Our projects have survived because of the continued hard work of our workers and an ability to accept the limitations of our own knowledge. I believe, as Camerawork's co-ordinator, that we have been success-ful, but this success has taken money, staffing, co-operation, networking, research, argument and sleepless nights. No one said it would be an easy process, but then no one knew what kind of process it would be!

Camerawork is proud to present the work of David Hevey. We believe *The Creatures Time Forgot: Photography and Disability Imagery* will prove to be a landmark in the struggle for alternative imagery and empowering processes. Perhaps more than most, David Hevey has been a pioneer in visually articulating the state of the disability movement and its challenges to oppressive imagery. Camerawork is proud to have played its role in this struggle.

DAWN LANGLEY

Acknowledgements

From the disability movement, I would like to thank Rachel Hurst, the Campaign to Stop Patronage, Vicky Waddington, Allan Sutherland, Michael Turner, Liz Crow, Rosalie Wilkins, Sian Vasey, Chris Davies, Colin Barnes, Raina Haig, Mary Duffy, Stephen Millward, Brian Jenkins, Micheline and Lucy Mason, Vic Finkelstein, Mike Oliver, Ailsa Fairley, Roger Symes, Maria Barth and CLIC, Ruth Collett and Invalid, Carolyn Lucas, Jane Campbell, Kath Gillespie, Natalie Markham, Jenny Morris, Anne Macfarlane, the National League of the Blind and Disabled, the Greater Manchester Coalition, the London Borough's Disability Resource Team and the Greater London Association of Disabled People. I would like to express my appreciation to fellow members of the BCODP Media Images Sub-Group and to the many organisations, disabled or non-disabled, who invited me to discuss my work and refine many of the arguments in this book. A special thanks to Elspeth Morrison, editor of *Disability Arts in London*, for providing me with much material and many ideas.

I would like to thank Harvest Information Service, in particular Joanne Lawrence; Bushy Kelly and Sue Isherwood of the Arts Council; *Disability Arts in London* magazine; *Link Magazine*; Durrants Clippings Agency; Susan Scott-Parker; Amanda King and Nina Patel from GLA; BBC 2's *One-In-Four*, in particular Chris Hutchins; the Charities Aid Foundation for valuable talks and key documents; the King's Fund Centre library; *Campaign* magazine; Ian Williams, author of *The Alms Trade: Charities Past, Present and Future*; also, Roger Symes, Anne Fairbairn and Freda Luffy for their support.

From the US and Canada, my thanks to Irving Kenneth Zola, Diane Driedger, the Disability Rights and Education Fund, the International Center for the Disabled, New

Langan Arts; also particular thanks to Judy Wieser and the Photo-Therapy Center, Vancouver, for the volumes of information and discussions.

From the Arts Council of Great Britain, I'd like to express my gratitude to the Photography Advisory Group for their funding support; also the Training Department for training grants and the policy and development section for conference grants. In particular, I would like to give a very special thanks to Barry Lane, the Arts Council Photography Officer, who supported the whole project, of which this book is a part, when it was merely an idea. He has displayed progressive and constant support throughout.

From the independent photography sector, I'd like to acknowledge the contribution made by Jessica Evans, lecturer in photography at PCL, for critical discussions on photographic theory. Also I'd like to thank Paul Wombell of Impressions; Terry Morden and Lorna Mills of the National Museum of Film and Photography; Roberta McGrath and Andy Golding from the Polytechnic of Central London Photography Course; the workers at Camerawork Gallery, particularly Dawn Langley.

For permissions from those who commissioned photography or those appearing in my photographs, in no particular order: from A Sense of Self, thanks to St John, Everton, Derek (RIP),Jane and the workers and to the others who took part in the photography sessions at the Effra Trust, Noski, Clair and Geraldine, Paul, Phillipa, Mike and Ellie (RIP). From Striking Poses, I'd like to thank the Graeae Theatre Company and the children of Richard Cloudesley and Franklin Delano Roosevelt schools. From Beyond the Barriers, I'd like to express my gratitude to St John Nightingale, Kath and her family, Chris, Clair, Geraldine (and Mac), and Andrew. From the miscellaneous shoots, I'd like to thank Adam, Micheline and Lucy, Max and the London Borough of Hammersmith, Laura and the London Borough of Camden, Gary of People First, the London Disability Arts Forum, Vaughn and the London Borough of Southwark, Sean and Community Service Volunteers, ILEA, Nick and the National Union of Civil and Public Servants. From *The Creatures Time Forgot* shoots, I'd like to thank my brother John, Gerry, my mother, Kay, Micheline and Lucy, Kath, Vince, Raina and Jenny, Sian Vasey, Heart 'n' Soul, Elspeth Morrison and Adam

Reynolds. I'd also like to thank the Construction Safety Campaign and the Institute of Education.

For permissions to reproduce charity posters, thanks to the Spastics Society, the MS Society, BMP DDB Needham, and Mencap.

I would like to convey my appreciation to those who read parts, chapters or the whole manuscript. These people did a tremendous, time-consuming job and provided me with valuable feedback. They are Helena Roden, Christine Hevey, Jo Spence, Dawn Langley, Mike Oliver, Gill Newsham and Sian Vasey.

Creatures Time Forgot: Photography and the Construction of Disability Imagery was crucially supported by Dawn Langley and the workers of Camerawork. Funding came from the Rowntree Foundation, the Arts Council of Great Britain, the Greater London Arts, Camerawork and Hoskyns PLC. I would particularly like to acknowledge the support of the Rowntree Foundation Disability Committee, from which the greater part of this financial support came.

From my publishers, I would like to thank Jane Armstrong, who supported the book when it was two sides of A4. I especially want to thank Rebecca Barden who saw *The Creatures* to fruition. She was clear, concise, supportive and friendly. Thanks also to Moira Taylor, Sandra Jones, Nigel Marsh and Alice Stoakley for their hard work and support.

A major acknowledgement must be made to the charity and ad agency personnel. Despite knowing the position that I would be taking on charity advertising, many people devoted much of their time to help me in my research. I conducted dozens of interviews (of which roughly half were anonymous and a half attributable). I have decided not to name any of the sources because, first, the issue is not about individuals or particular charities, and second, because I would not like the book, particularly its conclusions on charity advertising, to be used against those who were prepared to discuss the issue by those who were not. Those who gave time whether openly or anonymously know who they are and I deeply thank them.

I also thank Giovanni, Alfonso, Nina and John and the others at the Riva Cafe,

Borough High Street, for the daily prawn salad sandwich. An army of ideas marches on its stomach.

The greatest thanks of all must go to the people who put up with me while I wrote this book. I thank them from the bottom of my heart for tolerating my obsession, my hysteria, my nagging, my sulking, my panic and my ego. In particular, Helena Roden, Dawn Langley and Jo Spence for almost daily support in the task of making critical sense of a difficult terrain. Thanks to you all.

DAVID HEVEY

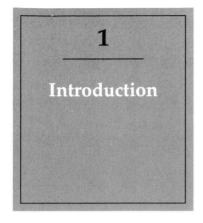

1

Introduction

I have had several flashes on the road to Damascus. The first came when, as a 15-year-old schoolboy, my chaos was compounded by the delirious, furious advent of an epileptic seizure. I did not know what it was and had probably never heard of epilepsy. Flashing lights, like bonfire sparklers with rainbow colours, appeared in front of my eyes. As I attempted to apologise to my grammar-school master for this inconvenience, my vision was almost totally eclipsed by this and the other hallucinations I was witnessing. I staggered into the playground out of his sight and into what I thought was oblivion.

For years I lived with this terror. At that period, the point about epilepsy was fear. It was, for me, the monotonous consistency of this terror and fear that made me 'an epileptic' all of the time, not just at the point of seizures. In fact, a curious alleviation of this fear came when I began to hallucinate and knew very well that I had about three minutes to get myself lying down and, even more daunting, settle down all those panicking around me. I very quickly realised that responsibility for my epilepsy had brought with it responsibility for other people's reactions: sometimes idiocy and ignorance, sometimes clear strength and support.

The second flash on this road to Damascus as a disabled person came when I encountered the disability movement. I had learnt to live with my private fear and to feel that I was the only one involved in this fight. I had internalised my oppression. As a working-class son of Irish immigrants, I had experienced other struggles but, in retrospect, I evidently saw epilepsy as my hidden cross. I cannot explain how significantly all this was turned around when I came into contact with the notion of the social model of disabilities, rather than the medical model which I had hitherto lived with. Over a matter of months, my discomfort with this secret beast of burden called epilepsy, and my festering hatred at the silencing of myself as a disabled person, 'because I didn't look it', completely changed. I think I went through an almost evangelical conversion as I realised that my disability was not, in fact, the epilepsy, but the toxic drugs with their denied side-effects; the medical regime with its blaming of the victim; the judgement through distance and silence of bus-stop crowds, bar-room crowds, and dinner-table friends; the fear; and, not least, the employment problems. All this was the oppression, not the epileptic seizure at which I was hardly (consciously) present.

As I worked to separate out the medical condition from the disability, I began to work on, even attack, the disabling areas. The first was the fifteen years which I had spent on toxic drugs. I am now working through a holistic health regime of homeopathy and cranial massage. No longer do I have to live with burning stomach pains caused by my toxic medication, no longer do I experience epilepsy as an area of shame and chaos. In coming out as a disabled person, the internalised phantoms have also come out: the 'hidden' medical condition is no longer hidden, at least by me.

My personal journey of private crisis, of the slow gaining of understanding of disability as an external oppression, and on into the disability movement, vitally informs my photographs. Although the photographic portraits tell a part of the story of those portrayed, the photographs also in part tell my story of transformation. Beyond the technical mechanics and processes, the real energy came from the interactive telling of stories from both sides of the camera. I like to feel that the re-creation of the release of energy and identity I felt on finding myself as a disabled person is fed into the often workshop-like situation of the photographic shoot.

This is not to say that the subjects were by any means passive beings waiting for illumination. The cross-identification between myself and the sitter/subject could not have worked if they themselves, as disabled people, were not aware personally and politically of their oppression. I have yet to meet the disabled person who was not aware, more or less, of his or her oppression, and it was often the working through of the sitter's desire to fight back which gave many of the images their energy. In a sense, that is all I have done. I have attempted to register photographically the energy in the fightback of individual disabled people and the disability movement.

When I was asked to produce a book of my photographs, it struck me that the offer was an ideal opportunity to put my work in the context of the wider personal and political disability arena. I have tried to address, therefore, some of the shifting sands that currently affect and govern disability imagery. Using my own work as the basis, this book is an attempt to explore the general disability imagery environment (or discourse) in which (or, more correctly, against which) my work exists.

The most infamous of these is charity advertising. But before entering the visual agenda, my approach has been to begin the exploration, in Chapter 2, of the presence and effect of the disability movement, and in particular the growth of what has become known as the social model of disability. This model, developed by disabled people, has come to be one of the main physical and theoretical tools of their fight for access and empowerment. The social model of disablement has to be understood, therefore, before we enter and examine the problematic images of the disability charities and the photography employed by charity advertising.

Charity photography is a form which is at once stubborn and fragile. A photography which, as I set out to demonstrate, is based on a medical view (or model) of disability cannot lead to the empowerment and liberation of disabled people. By looking at specific ads in the context of commercial and charitable advertising, and at the uneasy relationship between disabled people and charity imagery effected in our name, I aim to break away from the nihilism and negativity of this form of photographic representation. Chapters 3 and 4, then, deal with respectively the macro and the micro positions of charity representation.

Although charity advertising leads the field in negative representation of disabled people, it is by no means the only area of oppressive representation. In Chapter 4, I take a sample of other photographic 'uses' of disablement to create a general overview of these other areas of representation. By going in and below the surface (that is, examining the plastic image and the discourse[1] in which it exists) and by illuminating the hidden agendas at work within these images, I examine the intended role of these images and their effectiveness within the construction of notions of disability by non-disabled practitioners. Although the photographers whom I examine would doubt-less argue against, and possibly be shocked by, the links and continuities in their constructions of disability in photography, I believe that Chapter 5 demonstrates a widespread use of disabled people as 'other' for the consumption and alleviation of able-bodied fears, guilt and collusion in the oppression. The range of photographers examined is from the super-sensitive, soft left of Britain to the manic enfreakers of American photojournalism. The clear link is that these images have been constructed in the void created by the segregation of disabled people from all areas of social entry (not simply photographic self-representation). However, there are other more 'pro-active' links existing between these diverging genres and practices. I aim to show how these projections into this segregationist void tell more about the producers of the images, both individually and as a genre, than about the specific people portrayed. I will not be simply damning those who created the Damned – a sort of checklist of notoriety descending down to Diane Arbus and beyond – but I shall link them together, for the first time, as a loose group or genre in order for us to view these oppressive photographic constructions and their cultural currency for what they are, not for the ideal they aspire to.

Chapter 6 marks the point in the book where, the de-biologisation and de-medicalisation of disability imagery having been laid out and interpreted, we must ask about the next step. 'The disabled' have been examined in the representational custody of others, but if the point, as Marx said, is to change the world – in this case, the world of disability imagery – how might this be achieved? Having set what I consider to be the general oppressive agenda, I return to the original purpose of the book: my own work.

I would argue that there is no such thing as cultural production which is not *essentially* autobiographical, to a lesser or greater extent. The ridiculous notion that 'objectivity' can exist outside consciousness pervades much critical practice. Objective cultural practice has always sought to hide the person from the text. Cultural produce is considered 'subjective' and a lesser beast if scholastic conjecture becomes entwined with personal need and personal politics. Despite the feminist criticism that 'objectivity' is, in reality, male subjectivity, there is still a class and academic snobbery over the value of the pure word against the engaged word, the pure image against the engaged image. Art is the one area of bourgeois civilisation which is allowed to exchange pure objectivity for pure (still apolitical) subjectivity. A man may create huge womb-like paintings, as long as men's womb-envy of women is not named *politically*.[2] Another example: one may admire the greatness of Shakespeare, as long as the work is not read as the metaphorical biography of the real 'Shakespeare', that is, Edward De Vere, the 17th Earl of Oxford (1550-1604) and (along with all the others) lover of 'the virgin queen', Elizabeth I. As long as you subscribe to the 'Stratford Man' theory of Shakespeare, it becomes impossible to read Shakespeare as essentially magic-realist autobiography.[3] The lesson within bourgeois culture is obvious. The naming of the self (something impossible to avoid in cultural forms), and the naming of the *political* self in cultural theory and practice, is an unavoidable concomitant of an individual's struggle against his or her own brand of oppression. Nevertheless the intrusion of the self remains a controversial issue. In outlining my disability photography, I very firmly *subject*ify my work to the context of my self and my identity.

Furthermore, I have too often read photographic theory which failed to pull itself back into visual form, and visuals which had no idea of a theoretical context or orbit. Both processes are flawed. Similarly, I have read much 'issue-based' theory which, while explaining the whys, did not deign to explain the hows of the political image-making process. While I would support the right of cultural workers to tell the story of their practice (rather than wait all their lives, possibly fruitlessly, for the cultural establishment against which they may have been struggling to validate them), there is no doubt that the explanations have sometimes taken the place of the images. In the final analysis, given certain contextual considerations, the images must do their own work.

In many ways Chapter 7 is the nucleus and cornerstone of the book. Through an exploration of photographic theory – looking in particular at the work of Victor Burgin, Allan Sekula and Jo Spence, which deconstructs and 'reads' photographic imagery at the point of surface and in relation to the discursive context – I explore ways in which we can take these theories and develop them into a theory of how we, disabled people, can change oppressive representation. Pulling these theorists (that is, those that appear to resist mobilisation in a political context) into the *realpolitik* of the disability movement and its own position on oppressive representation, I look at how far these theoretical tools can help shift the representation agenda towards a general disability photographic practice.

To develop a theory of practice, however, I examine not just photographic theory, but drama theory. Looking at the 'post-Aristotelian' drama of tragedy, I look at the routes of the tragic drama. Drama theory and practice from Brecht to Augusto Boal and beyond have engaged in representation which breaks with the 'tragedy principle' of classic, that is apolitical or anti-political, drama. The struggle between *tragic* drama and *mobilised* (i.e. that which has a political task) drama echoes many of the struggles between reactionary and progressive cultural forms. However, this struggle in drama is perhaps the most vital for disability representation because the struggle against Aristotelian drama is predicated on its *tragedy thesis*. I argue that it is crucial that we connect this battle of the tragedy principle in drama to the politics of disability photographic representation.

It is from this terrain that I bring my work in this book to a close by outlining some possibilities for a model of disability imagery production using theories from radical drama to theories of the subject. How the observed begin their own observing is a crucial question in all radical cultural practice and its relevance is critical for new disability photographic practices.

The book closes with two further perspectives on disability representation. The first, by Jo Spence, takes the form of an interview and explores how her political and theoretical consciousness of herself as a cancer patient informs her working-tool of photography. Paradoxically, Jo Spence would describe her work as 'no big deal', by which she means that it does not primarily address discourses of either high theory or high art. Although her work is informed by a wide range of theories, its value as photographic practice is as a map of her entry into the cancer machine. She specifically brings her work on herself into the public arena to show how we can represent our own struggles. Jo Spence has consistently argued that in going public with her photography, she has in fact *added* to the struggle for survival as someone with cancer, because her work takes on the discourses of medicine and health *and* that of the photographic establishment. 'People caught up and fighting within the health and medicine discourses have constantly told me that the work has been useful for them. Within the photographic and representational discourses, however, the only direct comment I received was at an opening of an exhibition of my cancer work, when a person came up to me and said how much they liked the green frames!' Jo Spence's work offers to the disability movement and its allies a radical form of representation because she is herself inhabiting her representations.

Chapter 9 is the work of Jessica Evans (working with Andy Golding). Her work and theory come from a position of close proximity to the issue of mental or learning disablement. She has developed theories and practices of the representation of mental disablement on both the personal and the political levels. In this sense, her work is not the abstract wish of a non-disabled ally, but a serious critical contribution to change. Her piece explores the construction of mentally disabled people within both historical and representational terms. She examines how the visual constructions of the Mencap charity adverts, in particular, contain the marks of wider and more powerful discourses affecting mental disabilities. Again, like Jo Spence, her photographs work on the methods of constructed documentary, rather than the classic naturalist representation of mental disabilities, which she critically attacks.

Disabled people have had more images launched in their name than Helen ever had ships. Despite the gains made and the pressures exerted by the disability movement, non-disabled photographers and cultural organisations of all political hues still take upon themselves, and therefore away from disabled people, the mission to capture 'disability' photographically. Morally, of course, it is not permissible for them to admit to this imperialist tendency. Much liberal hand-wringing 'equal opportunities' rhetoric is aired and descends, like an old London fog, to hide all in a pea-souper of rhetoric, right-on-ness and smugness. 'People with disabilities' are to be admitted but only with the ball and chain of 'disabilities' still firmly attached to their bodies.

8   The creatures time forgot

Despite the pressure and educative efforts of the disability movement, for most photographers the words 'impairment' and 'disability' remain synonyms.

Disabled people are visually needed, but as metaphorical symbols for other meanings and practices. Who better to do this than those with apparent bodily differences? Consistently, 'left' photojournalism has created sub-genres on the back of a general 'species' construction, but all those flights to the famines to make a reputation are expensive. So, if you can't afford to get to Africa, what about an inner-city day centre? This photo-surveillance by non-disabled photographers of disabled people crosses most positional and ideological barriers and is in danger of becoming an epidemic. The presence and pressure of the disability movement has meant that arts funding bodies in particular are prioritising disability and in turn pressurising their client organisations to 'do the disabled'. In a word, the political gains of the disability movement have paradoxically created a growth in the presence of 'disability' imagery in a number of competitions, exhibitions and magazines. The growth of consciousness of the issue of disability has led to an increase in the incidence of oppressive representation.[4]

I do not pretend to be conclusive in the exploration of a counter-image, but I believe it is imperative that the disability movement develop methods to influence image-making from the inside and the outside. Only then can we begin to create a disabled-led agenda for the production of disability photographic imagery to suit the attendant growth of the disability access movement.

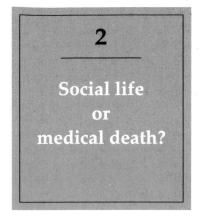

2

Social life
or
medical death?

Impairment: Lacking part of or all of a limb, or having a defective limb, organism or mechanism of the body.

Disability: The disadvantage or restriction of activity caused by a contemporary social organisation which takes no or little account of people who have physical impairments and thus excludes them from the mainstream of social activities.[1]

While an explosion of images of disabled people (with few actually *by* disabled people) has hit our recent media consciousness, with three of the latest Oscar-winning films focusing upon disability,[2] concerned organisations in the UK have responded with seminars exploring how we can change negative images of disabled people. Disappointingly, these have promised more than they have delivered, particularly for disabled people, since the seminars and conferences have invariably been predicated on a profound misunderstanding of what disability actually is.[3]

A typical seminar might be conducted something like this: coffee and registration; opening session and keynote speech by great, good or worthy person-of-power; two more speeches by middle-to-low importance government officials; final speech by a conspicuous, but politically safe, disabled 'consultant'; break for coffee.

Workshops are divided into groups according the prearrangements of the conference organiser. Workshop titles may include Sector Group Information Sharing, How Best to Show People with Disabilities, Ability Not Disability, Disability Etiquette, Labelled Disabled, and so on. The non-disabled majority of workshoppers are bustling and keen, although the disabled presence – already small in the opening plenary – has been further divided into the workshops. The non-disabled-dominated workshop discussion begins and is steered by a non-disabled 'facilitator' (given services free, old boy) who will orchestrate the not-so-hidden agenda. The facilitator will throw out verbal boomerangs which, when they return correctly, will be written up on the ubiquitous flipchart. The disabled people will try to make interventions (will we have to shout and scream at them or will they sprout brains?) which will be softened up by the time these comments pass through the workshop facilitator's thick pen on to the flipchart. After being the object of the non-disabled guilt and fury at our disabled rejection of their non-disabled constructions, we will all gratefully break for tea.

The disabled people will meet together and the non-disabled people will meet together. Some of the non-disabled people will approach us and try to soften what we said into what they think we *really* meant, and get hurt by the obvious fact that we mean what we say. Still others will approach and tell us, *sotto voce*, how much they agreed, or how impressed they were, but that they couldn't bring it up/ commission a poster campaign/rewrite their equal ops policy because the director/ board/management committee/old so-and-so (delete where appropriate) prevents them taking action. And when they find that their confession has not absolved them from the disabling situation, they will withdraw their confession and turn back to rage.

The rest of the seminar, for disabled people, will be a slow decline. The day will draw to a close with a feedback session, with the facilitator reporting back a four-sentence summation of our workshop's conclusions on 'How to Represent People with Disabilities'. The chair of the day will be gracious enough to allow one of the disabled people from the same workshop five seconds to scream objections at the facilitator. This pattern will see the day safely to a close, with each facilitator 'reporting back' the once-hidden, now open agenda. Like Orpheus returning from the Underworld, the journey will have promised much but delivered nothing. Disability will still be located exclusively in the body, not in the environment. The end will have finally come, and the non-disabled conference organiser will heave a self-satisfied sigh of relief at having prevented the disabled people present from 'hijacking' what should have been their forum.

Disabled people will have made interventions and attempted to make their viewpoints clear. We may have even won over numerous allies, but the host organisation machine will grind on. The chair of the day will sum up, invariably by contexting this issue into the greater cosmos of the problems and survival of the organisation.[4] No firm pledges will have been given and no concrete steps will have been laid out. In the final analysis, the exercise was one of 'attitude change' and not replanning. As for any new ways of creating images of disabled people that might result from any 'trickle down' effect of these seminars (and it is still too early to judge their relative success), they are likely to show disabled people not as chronically unconscious dependants (or monsters) but more as grinningly happy dependants (or monsters). Richard III with a face-lift? 'Positive' images of 'people *with* disabilities', from this point of view, will doubtless show them enjoying their oblivion.

Disabled people are likely to have witnessed the charade not as a contribution to the liberation of disabled people at the level of representation, but as a part of the resistance to change. The attenders from the ad agencies and charities will return to the process of non-disabled image-making, beginning and ending with a non-disabled photographer, directed by non-disabled art director, commissioned by non-disabled-employing ad agency, working for non-disabled-controlled charity, appealing to the (assumed to be) non-disabled public. The only possible contribution from the disabled subject of this entire process is likely to be the change of facial muscles from a grimace to a grin.

To call it superficial is a compliment and much if not most disability representation and imagery initiatives, including seminars, conferences, commissions and so on, make the consistent mistake of seeing the beginning of reforming disability imagery *solely* within the four corners of the image. Images of disabled people are then seen as free-floating self-referential visual *facts* with no particular past or future – they exist only in the here and now. Obviously, given that the disability charities have historically been one of the main agents of representational (let alone organisational) oppression of disabled people in their advertising, they will be less than keen to context their imagery within the wider disability discourse or power equation.

However, the task in hand is to illuminate this discourse that surrounds and controls particular forms of disability image construction *before* we re-enter the Jericho wall of disability imagery and disability imagery making.

Many people shiver at the very notion of entering a theoretical discourse. The very word itself, like 'bourgeois' in the late 1970s, is in danger of dying through overuse, particularly within the issue-based independent photography sector. Currently, when the disability imagery debates have arisen, these have invariably been predicated upon finding a simple solution to the somewhat spurious dialectic of negative versus positive imagery which has, in reality, been a debate between different forms of *impairment* photography and the issue of ethics therein. Charities (whom I cite regularly because they are by far the largest producers and distributors of oppressive impairment/negative disability imagery – see Chapters 3 and 4) in particular have been extremely reluctant to accept a recontexting of the debate on disability imagery away from impairment-fixation problem-in-the-body imagery. This is hardly surprising because, although they are called 'disability' charities, they are in fact *impairment* charities. One only has to read the names – the Multiple Sclerosis Society, the Spastics (sic.) Society, the British Epilepsy Association, Imperial Cancer, etc. – to see this.

In this sense, then, debates about correct and incorrect, positive or negative, empowering or disempowering disability photographic imagery will continue to flounder and sink into nothingness if we do not first go briefly outside the imagery and examine how disability itself has come to exist. Only in this way can we disentangle the apparent web of misnaming and mismeaning within the representation of this phenomenon.

Within general disability representation, it is clear that it is the impaired body of the disabled person on to which is projected the negative manifestations of that impairment in society: that is, the disability. In this way, characters like Richard III, Frankenstein, Graham Greene's Raven,[5] most villains in the James Bond films and so on, have their evilness signified by their impairment.[6] As these stories unfold, the anti-hero's limited and semi-human consciousness glimpses their tragic existence through the cracked mirror of their hatred for themselves. They all live bitterly with the festering sore of their loss, until their self-destructive rage explodes on to the world. The built world of civilisation in turn facilitates their civilisation-saving deaths. Like that of Lenny in John Steinbeck's *Of Mice and Men*,[7] their death is civilisation's final altruistic act of kindness (despite the provocation). Civilised society has saved itself because it is just that – civilised – and the anti-hero is dead because he could not live with his personal tragedy. A (meta)physical-impairment drama is complete.

That disablement is centrally viewed as personal tragedy and loss within the body, there can be no doubt. This personal tragedy theory of disability is in turn supported by ideologies feeding into it or adjusted from this to suit different environments. At its core, as Oliver has pointed out,[8] stand three implicit and historical theories of disability. The first suggests that in societies dominated by religious or magical ways of thinking, impairment may be perceived as a punishment from God or from evil magic. The second 'implicit underpinning'[9] is based on a theory of 'liminality' which views

> the long-term physically impaired [as] neither sick nor well, neither dead nor fully alive, neither out of society nor wholly in it. They are human beings but their bodies are warped or malfunctioning, leaving their full humanity in doubt. . . . The disabled spend a lifetime in a . . . suspended state. They are neither fish nor fowl; they exist in partial isolation from society as undefined, ambiguous people.[10]

The final and third 'underpinning' of the personal tragedy view of disability, Oliver argues, is the 'surplus population thesis' which manifests itself in societies where economic survival is a constant struggle. Therefore any weak, impaired or old people who threaten this survival by their (apparent) unproductivity are either killed at birth or left to die.

Oliver's work takes these implicit theories apart and, quoting Abberley, describes these three underpinnings of the personal tragedy theory as 'a particular kind of descriptive anthropology which sees societies as, in the final analysis, the embodiment not of social and economic relationships but of *thought systems*'.[11]

So far, the manifestations of personal tragedy theory, in attempting to outline 'attitudes' to disabled people, do not explain the historic growth of disablement (though they may be unwittingly registering their complicity with a disabling society). We have to look at the work of disabled theorists like Finkelstein and Oliver to find this.

Finkelstein was the first disabled social scientist to put down a theoretical framework for shifting away from the personal tragedy or medical view of disability, consolidated by institutions and professions built up by this notion, to a view of disability as a social construction based on (the lack of) *access*. His key text for the World Rehabilitation Fund, entitled *Attitudes and Disabled People*,[12] was labelled by one of its critics, somewhat derisively, as 'a political manifesto',[13] although that is precisely what it is. However, it does not contain a set of demands for disability rights, as such, but an analysis of the nature of disabling oppression.

Finkelstein was commissioned to write the monograph, as the title suggests, to examine attitudes to disability and disabled people. However, it was clear from the outset that in this brief he was expected to examine attitudes as a specific and separate force, and presumably the potential for attitude change, in this case in the world of rehabilitation, outside of any historical-materialist framework.[14] Finkelstein rejected this notion of attitude-change, which owes much to a Hegelian idea of thought as a primal force shaping the material world before it. The logical conclusion of this viewpoint is that the material world (for disabled people, the material world of physical inaccessibility) is taken as given and fixed and is an afterfact of the world of attitudes and ideas. In order truly to understand attitudes to either impairment or disablement from a definite historical-materialist viewpoint, Finkelstein abandoned this as a starting point and instead outlined what he called the three historical phases of disability.

Phase one, as Finkelstein saw it, existed in the feudal, pre-Industrial Revolution period. At this time 'cripples', as Finkelstein calls disabled people of this phase, were not separate from society. They were not segregated from society or their social class in any way that we would recognise today, for example, in institutions or by receiving particular services. They existed at the lower end of the economic ladder and formed a broad oppressed layer along with low-paid workers, the out-of-work, the mentally ill and so on, and there were broad overlaps within this group. According to Finkelstein, there was no 'disabled' group as such, since the systematic social exclusion of impaired people from economic production had not yet begun.

Phase two, Finkelstein continues, begins to grow with the Industrial Revolution and its creation of new productive technology within large-scale industry. Here the production lines were geared to able-bodied norms based on clear assumptions of a more or less constant notion of labour-power within individual and collective workers. As the Industrial Revolution consolidated its power, hired 'hands' competed for work within systematic production lines whose time-as-money norm excluded the difference of those with physical impairments. Phase two proper, however, was 'inaugurated' with the growth of asylums and institutions to deal with the growing destitution of those with impaired labour power. The charities consolidated this process of identification of types of non-labour givers by differentiating between the deserving poor (those who could not work in the new production lines) and the undeserving poor (those who were presumed to be able but idle). The disabled were now in place and that place was segregated. In segregating disabled people from a work-based community to a needs-based institution, the notion of dependency was put in place.

The creation of segregated institutions for disabled people in turn facilitated the growth of attendant impairment specialist workers, or the disability professions. Since disabled people were in these non-productive institutions, it became only natural that these professions would be geared to cure-or-care programmes in an effort to adjust disabled people into labour-givers (capital now having reduced the mass of people into vessels of labour power). The large-scale institutions, ranging during this phase-two period from colonies and asylums to hospitals and segregated schools, created the environment for a growth of physiotherapists, occupational therapists, social workers, counsellors, etc. These, Finkelstein asserts, themselves became dependent on the existence of the 'dependent' disabled.

We are then beginning to see, within phase two, the growth of what Finkelstein called *the disability paradox*, which is the relationship between a person (and his or her impairment) and the state of society (the social restrictions imposed upon the individual). Sometimes passive, sometimes in conflict, the paradox is in the relationship between the two. The demarcation line of this paradox itself shifts because while the incarceration and segregation of impaired people created the group called disabled people, it also facilitated developments in health care which in turn ensured that greater numbers of people with impairments would survive. That notwithstanding, phase-two attitudes and organisations are characterised by the gaze of society being upon the person with an impairment, not on the social disablement.

However, in *phase three*, which Finkelstein believes is happening now, the stage is being set for a shift in the position of disabled people and a shift in this gaze. As Finkelstein puts it, 'In phase two the focus of attention is firmly on the physically impaired individual. In phase three the focus is the nature of society which disables physically impaired people.'[15]

Finkelstein singles out in particular the decline in heavy manufacturing and the growth of the electronics-based industries and the attendant new technology. This, as he sees it, enables even the most impaired person to operate environmental controls. That this technology is here, he concludes, means that new forms of relationships within the disability paradox must come about, leading to the 'elimination' of disability after the struggle to reintegrate impaired people into the community.

Finkelstein has been criticised for the simplicity of his historical analysis, particularly by disabled feminists who do not see the journey from the body-as-the-site-of-oppression to society-as-the-site-of-oppression as a simple matter of shifting ideological models of phase two to phase three. That notwithstanding, what both Finkelstein's and Oliver's work has clearly done is to create many of the theoretical conditions that have aided the physical growth of the disability movement today. Furthermore, it has become clear that whereas the medical professions, social sciences research, and charity advertising have used and constructed a medical and dependency view of disability *in which the impairment and the disability are both contained with the body*, disabled thinkers like Oliver and Finkelstein have *separated out the bodily impairment from the socially created disablement.*

The 'problem of disability' itself has now been opened up. Now we return to 'disability imagery'. Finkelstein's phase-two disability paradox, although a theoretical position, describes a reality that currently exists. Disability imagery, therefore, might be defined as the imagery that exists within the disability paradox. This is to say, disability photographic imagery is that which ranges from the representations of impairment to that which shows representations of the social oppression of disabled people. Negative or positive images produced within this discourse may be negative or positive about either side, the impairment or the social oppression. Also, their meanings as images may shift in time and context.

That disability imagery can comprise multiple viewpoints or gazes, ranging from the impairment and the body to the disabling social environment, is not yet clear to many people concerned with this area. At a recent conference where I was a guest speaker, a woman whose impairment was epilepsy said that she had come with an awful fear that I would show 'positive' images of people having seizures! People laughed at her honesty but her comment was far from daft. Her question seems to comprise many strands important to disability photographic representation: these have to be answered as much by developing a *process* of image production, as by the alternative single image. Her question embodied the unresolved dread at her condition; the as-yet unimaginable viewing of her impairment within a social model of disability; the fear of a 'positive' denial of her experience of terror in the seizure; and, finally, a lack of image references for her and others to call upon. In short, she had spoken an agenda which should challenge all disability photographic imagery. In the next chapter, we look at a type of disability photography which answers it the least.

3

The creatures time forgot

PART 1
INTO THE GROTTO OF
CHARITY ADVERTISING

Well, I wanted to find my self and my sort, so I went along to the British Epilepsy Association's local group meeting. I walked in and I knew straight away who was who. All those sitting in the chairs facing the chairwoman were epileptics but the lady conducting the proceedings most definitely wasn't. I listened for as long as I could stand to her controlling the meeting, telling people with epilepsy what to do, how to swallow a pill and so on, then I got up angrily and demanded, 'Are you actually an epileptic?' and she said, 'No, but my dog is'.[1]

There are over 170,000 registered charities in the UK,[2] the top 200 of which have a combined voluntary income of over £1 billion.[3] Of these, the 'medicine and health' charities, which include 'deaf, blind, chest and heart, physically handicapped, and cancer' and so on,[4] are the biggest single grouping and receive around a third of this income. The next biggest group of charities within the top 200 receive donations to a total of £300 million, and this grouping includes charities concerned with ex-service people, the elderly, welfare by religious groups, children and others: these too are likely to contain substantial areas of provision for disabled people.[5] If the league table of charity voluntary income, or 'giving', is widened to look at the 200–400 leading charities in the league, the percentage of impairment charities approaches 50 per cent of the total voluntary income.[6] If charity is big business, impairment charity is the biggest.[7]

Ever since Band Aid led the charge of the light entertainments brigade into charity, the 1980s have been and will be viewed as the decade in which, as Diana Leat has written, broadcasters first recognised the attractions of charity appeals.[8] This was more than *Stars on Sunday*, it was stars all day and half the night all over the globe.

These events appeared as pure altruism by the beautiful people, not narcissism gone mad (though many of the 'stars' were well past their sell-by date). This was the dawning of the mega Good Cause funded by a caring citizenship. Thank goodness! Although Band Aid was organised for relief of the Ethiopian famine of 1984, it set the tone and direction for a veritable litter of appeals which all included a substantial 'concern' for disabled people, including Comic Relief, BBC Children in Need, Live Aid and Thames Telethon. At the level of representation at least, these 'spectaculars' appeared to lead the way to a new, improved, caring culture: a culture which not only appeared to flourish in the midst of capitalism, but which appeared to be a viable substitute for the impersonal and decreasing state provision.

However, a closer reading of the statistics gives quite a different picture. Take Thames Telethon 1988. The total requested sum of the grant applications to the Telethon 1988 fund was £241,991,085. Of this sum, less than a tenth (£22 million) was actually raised by the event.[9] Furthermore, the financial applications from organisations 'dealing with' disability alone were more than five times the total funds available.[10] It was out of its depth. A final note which has been observed by the Charities Aid Foundation[11] is that these high-profile, day-long events raise total sums which, on average, are in any case raised *every day* for charity. In fact, in the UK, taking the sum of the entire voluntary donations given to the UK charitable sector, these events often raise *less* per day (i.e. per event) than the national daily average! Clearly, on any criterion and from any position, 'spectaculars' can't even do what they set out to do, let alone come anywhere near servicing the real needs of disabled people, but who ever thought that these events could?

Well, the three-times elected Thatcher Conservative government, which dominated the 1980s, believed they might. Thatcherism attempted to promote credit-consumerism as the point-of-consumption engine ('late capitalism') which would pull point-of-production British manufacturing out of its slow death. This was accompanied by the cultural promotion of 'active citizenship' to replace the individual's taxed responsibility for state and social provision which, it was argued, suppressed the customer's right to choose how to spend his/her own wages. Furthermore, there was to be no such thing as society, only collections of individuals and families. The non-socially constricted active citizen within the Tory vision of New Age capitalism could both own and care with choice. They could own a part of the production, through privatised share issues of ex-nationalised industries, and, as their wealth was supposed to rise and their taxes fall, they had a free choice to care (or not) at the point of consumption, by donating in response to appeals on the TV or in the underground.

Thatcher had been elected on a platform of rolling back the frontiers of the state (as well as solving the UK's economic and efficiency problems). In promoting tax-cuts-as-freedom, Thatcher's radical (that is, unfettered and Victorian) capitalism in turn attempted to starve the monolithic 'Nanny' state by controlling the UK money supply and with almost religious fervour doing battle with the public sector borrowing requirement. Victory would pave the way for the organisations which were voluntary and non-statutory and therefore able to respond far more quickly to needs on the ground. These expanded non-statutory organisations were supposed to feed off society (as a group of individuals) in a simple payments/donations for services equation.

The vision was of a Britain without conflicting private and public sectors but with private-for-profit and private-for-non-profit sectors in ideological harmony. This shift away from public provision to voluntary or private 'giving' was underpinned by a number of legal reforms affecting tax concessions, payroll giving, covenants and so on.[12] Into the centre of this legal, economic and ideological web was supposed to fit the answer to all needs, the 'cardinal litmus test of the enterprise culture':[13] the active citizen. It was their support, given either altruistically or in accordance with their own needs, which would fuel the economic transformation of social provision away from rights into privacy or charity.

However, it has been observed[14] that while total turnover of UK charities in 1987 was £12–£13 billion, including charities' own investment income and statutory contributions from central and local government, and income from fees and services and so on, only £2 billion or £3 billion was attributable to actual voluntary giving. When this is compared to the central government final consumption figures for the nation's health in 1988 of £22,346 million (i.e. ten times the total voluntary donations to all UK charities),[15] not only do we see how ridiculous is the task set the 'active citizen', it also becomes clear that this person-of-straw was an ideological fantasy whose existence was crucially dependent on the media's uncritical acceptance of the potential for individual giving. In a word, it was at the level of representation that the ideological fantasy of charity giving and charity success was made to appear real.

Furthermore, there were other political reasons why the charity-active-citizen apex was promoted. The apparent custodians of the new caring culture, the voluntary charitable organisations, were and are legally barred from political action[16] and therefore could be directed away from the political agendas which had grown up in the local authority-assisted voluntary sector of the 1970s. They would not be concerned with political rights, they would only be concerned with charity. In case anyone didn't understand this, guidelines were published and the ground-rules were spelled out in the press and media: 'The role of the charity is to bind up the wounds of society. This is what they get their fiscal privileges for. To build a new society for someone else.'[17] If people were still in any doubt, the 1989 White Paper stated that 'The powers and purposes of a charity should not include the power to bring pressure to bear on the government to adopt, to alter or to maintain a particular line of action.'[18]

Finally, as Ian Williams has put it, the subtext to this driving of statutory and voluntary provision out of the control of the state was 'a conviction that large nationalised bodies give the unions too much power. The atomisation of the service achieves the diffusion of that power.'[19] Organisations within the public sector that had been historically organised by their constituency groups for rights and power, like the trade unions, were being circumvented in favour of the voluntary sector charities which, many argue, not only were not organised by their constituency groups, but indeed were organised for their constituency groups' dis-empowerment – and the biggest single bloc of these organisations in terms of voluntary income and public consciousness[20] is the impairment/disability charities.

Given the enormity of the task set them, many charities may have felt extremely ambivalent about the responsibility and position which was being forced upon them by the government. Nevertheless, they were heavily implicated in the process. The

Spastics Society, for example, led the consortium that bought out Tadworth Children's Hospital, which transferred out of the NHS in 1983. As Tim Yeo is quoted as saying, 'We actually provided a model for this whole opt-out procedure long before anybody thought of it.'[21] However, this 'privatisation' of the children's hospital brought with it attendant problems. Tadworth Court, on going independent, did not get any of the £16 million from the sale of some of the land for housing[22] and the Spastics Society found it very difficult to raise the funds, which pressured them to adjust fees. David Brindle in the *Guardian*[23] found that only 13 per cent of the income from the venture was being raised by appeals and donations, as fee-paying as a part of revenue grew in significance. At the bottom of this heap are, of course, the users. Clearly, the pressure was on to raise charges to disabled users.

Only now do we get a glimmer of what this entire process might mean to disabled people. Throughout this drive to create charities as the replacement of the state as provider of key services, there has been practically no questioning at all of the assumption that charities automatically speak for their constituent or 'user' group. In taking the phase-two attitudes and structures as given, the 'disability' charities have created a hegemony, a near totality, in which their voice is accepted as *the* voice of disabled people. Within the disability industry, however, disabled people are actually the last in line. The hegemony has meant that the 'dependency' of disabled people on charity (and not the other way round) has been read as absolute. Therefore, the ideology or social position of charities within the disability paradox is hidden behind the mask of total altruism.

Even more importantly, outside the disability movement (itself the only real challenge to the 'disability' industry),[24] there has been practically no questioning *whatsoever* of the construction and representation of disabled people as impairment carriers by the impairment-specific charities.[25] The impairment as disablement sleight is critical. Charities, in their advertising, have constructed an identity for themselves and for their particular brand of impairment based on a number of both hidden and open assumptions. Seeing the development of the medical (cure-or-care) view of disability, some of the image purposes and assumptions are relatively clear: disabled people inhabit a living social death in a bone-cage bodily oblivion which is not of their own making. Inside the advertising image they are cripples, they are handicapped, they cannot function or work. Their position is that of the deserving poor. Suspended within the charity poster, they are neither in nor out of society.

Outside the advertising image, the Great Out There is the YOU who have your bodies (or so this advertising is designed to convince you). You are the 'public', you can enter 'public' (i.e. inaccessible) toilets and public (again, inaccessible) transport.[26] You must give what you own in order *not* to get what they have! In your fragile freedom, these sub-mortal specimens appeal to your able-bodiment and all its apparent privileges. You are here and now – in an underground station, reading your paper, watching the TV – but they, those creatures time forgot, float in a flotsam of despair. Charities defend the defenceless, don't they? The position is simple: you are being asked to give money or time or, most likely, both.[27] But you must give *something*. That then is the open agenda of charity advertising. Impairment is disability and disability is a neither dead nor living oblivion and this lost-in-(advertising)-space darkness would deepen still more if YOU did not give. This is the voice of the impairment industry, we know that your fears can hear us!

This is the representational produce of one of the major arms of the disability industry. It is important to make clear the difference between the disability industry and the disability movement. The disability industry is an impairment industry (ranging from the charities to the Department of Health and beyond) which has developed a weights-and-measures body-reading system to assess levels of impairment *as the level of disablement*. The percentage of impairment is read as the percentage of dysfunction or loss which in turn is the 'disablement'. The notion of loss (not of access) pervades phase-two attitudes and is visually anchored and made visually public in the high ground of charity advertising. Here we begin to uncover one of the many two-headed coins or the double binds of disability representation. The first side comprises the enforced anonymity or segregation (phase two) of disabled people through the disability apartheid system of 'needs-based' institutions, 'special-needs' schools, hospitals and so on. It is in these buildings and attendant professions that the social excommunication or absence of disabled people is made solid. Conversely, the other side of this double bind is that disabled people have a voiceless, powerless *hyper-presence* within charity advertising. Both sides of the coin, the institutions and the advertising, are 'for' disabled people but neither is controlled by them and both oppress them. Charity advertising serves as the calling-card of an inaccessible society which systematically segregates disabled people. It is the highest statement of segregation and it translates the actual segregation of disabled people into both a social and psychic reality by bonding the actual disablement of people with impairments with the psychic fear in non-disabled people of the loss of ownership of their bodies.

Charities have defended this process of disability image-building rather weakly by conceding that it produces pity and notions of dependency but arguing that pity is necessary for giving.[28] They have also developed a catch-22 argument that charity advertising constructs disabled people as dependent because this is an inherent function of disability charities! Moreover, those disabled people who are articulate and assured enough to criticise this, well they can't be disabled! Groups and people within the disability movement, like the Campaign to Stop Patronage and The BCODP Disability Media Images Group, have in turn attacked this form of imagery as 'negative' and oppressive. Although these groupings have yet to examine the construction of impairment/disability imagery in depth, they have at least begun to bring to the issue of charity advertising a controversy which it deserves. This is in marked contrast to the absence of disabled people's voices and the social view of disability in practically all other areas of 'concern' with charity and disability representation. This 'structured absence' of the disabled people and their organisations' challenges to appeals and advertising effected in their name is made clear in the following two cases.

The first is the thirteenth edition of *Charity Trends*,[29] the annual statistical and analysis publication by the Charities Aid Foundation. In reading this cover to cover, you will only be able to identify one paragraph in the 168 pages which mentions in any way the voice of disabled people. The author tells of the 'threat' of a challenge to charity appeals and advertising. It says:

Another threat comes from the increasingly vociferous lobby against such [charity] appeals. In reality the majority of objections are not directed specifically at broadcast appeals (although such appeals provide an excellent vehicle for publicity for objections) but are rather part of a more fundamental opposition to the role of charity in modern society. Insofar as this movement gains strength, the future of *all* charitable fundraising is in jeopardy. If the campaign for rights rather than charity [sic.] were allied with public disquiet about the increasingly blurred division between for-profit, not-for-profit and statutory provision, who can predict what the result might be?

It is worth quoting the paragraph extensively because, in conceding that 'the vociferous lobby against such appeals' exists, it nevertheless comes close, but ultimately fails to state that the genesis of this 'lobby' is from the largest group of apparent recipients, namely disabled people themselves. This Charities Aid Foundation piece is couched in the liberal language of concern for all, but is ultimately concerned with the survival of charities. Its claim that 'in reality' the majority of objections are not against appeals as such is completely unsubstantiated; while the closest it comes to acknowledging that a political struggle is being fought between disabled people and impairment charities (for whom Telethons are actually staged) is in the somewhat facile remark about appeals providing 'an excellent vehicle' for protest against such appeals. Without actually saying so, this sentence refers to the much-publicised picket of Telethon 1990 by between 150 and 200 disabled demonstrators.[30]

These protesters were entering the representation issue from the social view of disablement and they had entered the representation debate with parodying humour. Banners read 'Piss on Pity' and 'Blinded and Crippled by Tragic Disease'. Visually impaired disabled activist and equality-trainer Mike Higgins sold matches and wore the simple banner 'BLIND'. The very act of this putting-ourselves-in-the-dirt humour confronts the pathetic subhuman-dependency victim image of disabled people which *all* charity events ultimately rely on. This form of disabled people's anarchic culture[31] is light-years ahead of non-disabled concepts of 'arts with disability'. Basket weaving be warned! The reclaimed bile of radical activism is not quite the safe activity that concerned people have in mind. Without an understanding of the social model of disability, of course, those concerned with justifying charity solutions to the disability 'problem' cannot hope to grasp these actions. *Charity Trends* generally, and the above paragraph in particular, cannot move outside its semi self-defined, semi government-defined parameters of disability as impairment/dependency. So the cited paragraph from *Charity Trends* sounds the alarm for a union of forces that it cannot quite name. The end has hiding behind it the unreconcilable conflict between charity as an agent of dependency which underpins the impairment industry (and which, after all, the CAF is partly organised to facilitate) and the disability movement as an agent of empowerment for disabled people.

The second example of the structured absence within representation of disabled people's attacks on charity impairment imagery (whether it be the imagery of the Telethon or of general charity advertising) is within the local and national press. During a six-month period, I collected all the cuttings from the regional and national press and magazines[32] that dealt with charity advertising. I gathered a total of forty-three articles of varying lengths and depths and a very interesting picture of the management of 'charity advertising' as a media issue emerges.

The underlying message was, predictably, that impairment charities speak for disabled people and that disabled people cannot speak for themselves. This phase-two assumption is so absolute, at this level of representation, that only two articles out of the forty-three even came close to questioning this hegemony. From this trunk of charity advertising press coverage came the branches and twigs of regularly recurring themes. Articles dealt with the 'good cause' of charity; with 'compassion', 'faith', 'cure' and 'care'; with how to give to charity; what tax concessions were being made available to charities' television advertising (e.g. moves to exempt them of VAT charges); the success or failure of 'active citizenship' and advertising; and so on. Like a tortoise, disabled people are constructed as having their shelter of charity permanently on their backs.

The two largest groups within the media clippings were articles concerned with the areas of, first, the professionalism of charity advertising, or 'the hard sell' and, second, the need for caution over 'shock tactics' in advertising. All these articles had clearly read the same press releases and, particularly in the former, *Charity Trends* is continually quoted as the source of statistical proof that voluntary giving is under pressure and may even be declining. Given this, charities are 'therefore' under pressure to expand, or at least generate more voluntary income. It follows that their advertising has to dump its 'amateurish' past and embrace its professional future. The articles then emphasise the benefits for charities of paying 'market rates' (£40,000–£50,000+) for 'top people' to 'head the PR' to do just that. It was initially surprising that the articles weighed in from the viewpoint not of the charities but of marketing, public relations and advertising. Indeed, it is the smirking, smug portraits of these image saviours which adjoin the pieces and it is their quotes, in the main, which warn charities to the point of chastisement that they 'had better get their act together'.

However, it became clear that the tail did indeed wag the dog. Charity 'spokespeople' more or less acquiesced in the 'professional' vision of their advertising destiny. This demonstrated that in getting reduced rates, from ad agencies, for example, the charities give up much, sometimes total, power to these 'benefactors'. Certainly, the power over the image of the impairment charity was considered to be with the agency (with the 'amateur' charity on a yes/no/'er' basis). It was also clear from these articles that many PR and advertising people saw their entry into charity accounts as a 'good thing' if it remained on *their* terms, which were that the brand (the impairment and 'its' charity) would be handled by experts and not by amateurs. This was a trivialisation of a much deeper problem (at least for the charities) that still worries the charities.[33] This is that perceptions of professionalism and market strength may not equal increased voluntary giving. Given that the income for many leading charities broke down, on average, into a nearly half and half division between voluntary income and earned income (57 per cent voluntary/43 per cent other),[34] many charities feel that if they are to 'up-market' their image and advertising in order to pursue a larger slice of the total giving resources available, while at the same time attempting to become more 'professional' and increase the number of services and fee-earning areas available, the two areas may conflict in the minds of the givers who may begin to see the charity as a singularly commercial business, albeit with charitable status and tax subsidies. It becomes clear, at the same time, that both the ad agencies and the charities were keen to mask a business image and both accepted the central need to promote the charity not as a business but as an organisation of voluntary givers. Becoming professional while espousing voluntary giving is a dilemma the impairment charities have yet to solve.

These articles dealing with the professionalism of charity marketing and advertising were followed closely, in early 1991, by a cluster of articles all dealing with the warning from the Advertising Standards Authority to charities about 'shock tactics' in advertising.[35] Interestingly, these drew forth a couple of letters in the national press from people working for impairment charities who pleaded that while the imagery was problematic, they didn't know how else to show how horrendous life was for 'their' disabled people. While I do not doubt the sincerity of many volunteers and professionals who take what Anne Macfarlane has called 'the tea-party route to the disability issue' – that is, they still confuse impairment with disability and therefore work within the impairment charities to alleviate the 'problem' of disability. Nevertheless, these two letters demonstrate the somewhat existential problem facing progressive people working within these charities, namely: 'How do you show impairment as disability positively?' The answer, of course, is that while the disability charities are organised upon impairment lines (the British Epilepsy Association, the Multiple Sclerosis Society, etc.) they are bound by their own construction to show impairment-specific imagery tied to dependency. While impairment imagery is not necessarily negative (see Chapters 8 and 9), it will *always* be a part of the oppression as long as the impairment is constructed as the disablement.[36] For charities to agonise over 'shock imagery' is a bit like (to use Karl Marx's joke about capitalists denying the size of their profits) the virgin admitting she had a baby but only a small one! Shock imagery is not only inherent in the process, it is the logic of the process too.

However, this area of 'shock images' brings us closer to the involvement of disabled people within the press – namely, articles which give space to disabled people's views on advertising carried out in their name. Perhaps the most encouraging was entitled 'Disabling the shock tactics'[37] and, although it names the disability movement and the individuals as 'disability protesters' while, on the other hand, interviewing extensively several individually named heads of the major ad agencies who hold impairment charity accounts, it none the less makes it clear that not only is there controversy over charity advertising, but that the controversy is being generated by *disabled people*. Furthermore, one of the two is a unique article in that it quotes a disabled spokeswoman from the British Council of Organisations of Disabled People. The article is the clearest expression to date that it is disabled people and their organisations who are challenging the impairment charities' advertising and its effects.

In areas like the press, the issue of disability representation is constructed 'naturally' as the internal concern of charities, not of disabled people. Moreover, deconstruction or critiquing of disability imagery, where it has occurred, has not been directed either into the mechanics of production (that is, how images are made and where they come from and go to) or, to any great extent, into the construction of meaning internally within the imagery. All the efforts of the media and the charitable organisations have been to turn the political discourse on disability imagery into, at best, a superficial debate on 'positive' or 'negative' imagery or liberal hand-wringing over 'shock' imagery. The very act of consulting disabled people to approve or disapprove of finished articles of images-for-advertising on a push-button positive/negative level shifts the issue still further from the real battlegrounds. We have to move away from the passive approval/disapproval of impairment images into a role as active creators/producers of disability images. First, however, we have to continue the journey, to borrow a metaphor from Che Guevara, into the belly of the beast.

4

The creatures time forgot

PART 2
OUT OF THE GROTTO

There is no doubt that before the 1980s and early 1990s (when pressures came to be exerted on charities to market competitively) impairment charity advertising unashamedly relied, for its portrayal of disabled people, on notions of eugenics and the eugenic inferiority of disabled people.[1] Eugenics was a pseudo-science prevalent in the Victorian age which only lost its credibility during the Second World War. It means literally 'good genes', and it advocated and explored the breeding out of inferior genes. It mobilised a version of Darwinism to prove that bodily characteristics were evidence of species-kind. That is to say, the eugenicists believed that the constitution of the genes created a biological certainty about the social worth and position of individuals, races or classes. More than this, the negative genes would manifest themselves in bodily distinctions. Thus was the basis for much of the Victorian categorisation photography which sought to prove that bodily difference entailed difference in the entire psychic and social behaviour and make-up. The body became the signifier of difference for disabled people, as it still is very much today in charity advertising. Much of the theory of eugenics, when it affected disabled people, was a rationalisation and institutionalisation of the segregation of disabled people into legislative action to 'solve' the 'problem' of the sub species of disabled people. The 'Final Solution' was to monitor and control 'legally' the sexuality and birth rights of many groups of disabled people. While the legislative backing of these attempts to breed disabled people out of existence are (nearly) a thing of the past, there are clear links (the charities might argue they are circumstantial) between the biologisation of the issue of disablement by the eugenicists and the *em-body-ment* of the issue of disablement within charity advertising. Eugenics may have slowly died as a social theory and it would appear to have no place within much modern charitable thought (if 'modern charitable thought' is not a contradiction in terms), but it clearly is and was a trend, if not a movement.

None the less, the notion of screening out 'negative' genes very much prevails in the research wing of the bloc of impairment charities. The major impairment charities spend large parts of their funds on research to alleviate the source of the 'disability' from society. The Muscular Dystrophy Society spends £2.3 million per year on research; the Arthritis and Rheumatism Council £7 million; and Imperial Cancer Research £32 million. It goes without saying that similar sums are not spent by these charities 'researching' the implementation of civil rights for 'their disabled'. The researching and screening out of negative genes is what the impairment charities mean by a 'cure'. Furthermore, as Ruth Hill has pointed out,[2] the priorities of the impairment charities are very heavily weighted in favour of 'cure' rather than 'care'. Taking the example of the Muscular Dystrophy Group's offshoot, the Joseph Patrick Memorial Trust, the Trust is the welfare grant-giving arm, which has only £276,000 to spend, as opposed to the Muscular Dystrophy Group as a whole which spends £2.2 million on research (and £286,000 on advertising).

Within representation, people like Jessica Evans and Ruth Collett have made strong attacks on the overt continuity of eugenics in the advertising of the charities who 'deal' with mental or intellectual impairments. That notwithstanding, since the 1980s, many impairment charities have retreated at least from the visual representation of disability as an expressed issue of eugenics and have developed their advertising on a number of fronts both on and off the body. These we now need to look at.

Most impairment charities have very small turnovers. They are equivalent in income to small or medium-sized companies and it is therefore inconceivable that those impairment charities with voluntary incomes at the lower end of the top 400 giving scale (say, about £500,000)[3] could pay for national advertising campaigns which potentially could cost over £1 million in hoarding space alone.[4] While it may be easier for the larger charities with voluntary income at around £40 million, all charities which use the medium of advertising rely very heavily on the 'goodness' of the media machine, particularly ad agencies.

Charity clients are viewed by benevolent ad agencies as being, to adapt another of

Marx's phrases, the heart of a heartless nation, the opiate of the handicapped. The ad agencies may cringe at the 'amateurishness' of charitable organisations in marketing, they may secretly feel that the charity client's introspective thinking appears to thwart the very campaign that they, as an agency, have been asked to launch,[5] but these agencies are prepared to donate substantial services free or at a reduced rate in order to 'do their bit' towards disablement. The notion of disabled people's total dependency on charity is so all-pervading that it appears inconceivable that the agency could even think of charging commercial rates to those guardians of the dependent, the charities. The consensus between the charities and the ad agencies who hold charity accounts is that the relationship is not fiscal, it is moral.[6] Time and time again in interviewing people from both sides of this relationship (the third side which is absent is, of course, disabled people),[7] the charity account was quoted as something 'to get your teeth into and to be creative with, something which isn't the usual can of beans. It's a product that counts and we want to do our bit to help.'[8]

Agencies like Young and Rubicam (who list among their clients Mencap and the British Epilepsy Association) are multinational and have turnovers against which the income of their charity clients pales into insignificance. For example, for the year ending 1988, the British Epilepsy Association had an annual turnover of £566,240, whereas Young and Rubicam UK had a turnover of £194,745,000.[9] Not only is the turnover of Young and Rubicam around *350 times bigger* than that of the British Epilepsy Association, it also amounts to approximately two-thirds of the total voluntary income received by impairment charities within the top 200! In addition, Young and Rubicam UK is a subsidiary of Young and Rubicam Inc., USA. The last reported turnover, in 1987, for the entire company was $735 million, though that figure is likely to be something like £600 million for the current (1991) year! It is not surprising therefore that the giver–benefactor relationship between ad agencies and impairment charities often displays a sometimes hidden, sometimes open master–slave power equation weighted very much in favour of the 'giver', that is, the ad agency. This relationship emulates the giver–recipient relationship which the charities themselves have fostered within their 'brand' of impaired persons. Disempowerment for some abstract notion of 'the common good' is inherent within charitable organisations, although the irony is not altogether lost on them.[10]

So an advertising campaign begins. The ad agencies have a tried and, for them, trusted method of seizing 'a piece of mind',[11] which they feel is necessary if the public is eventually to donate to their particular charity. This means that they have to build a campaign which 'fights for the public eye, the public ear and the public purse'.[12] This capture and consolidation of the 'piece of mind' is, for them, the whole purpose of charity advertising and is a process conducted over time and over many linked campaigns. This process of pushing the charity client into the individual and public consciousness may vary from agency to agency and from charity to charity but a three-tenets or three-stages 'model' of charity advertising operations clearly emerges in which, again, the charity is the minor player. All that the charity will really bring to this process is the consolidated notion that the impairment represents the disability and that it wishes to dominate its particular impairment market. This is their 'corporate' strategy. For example, there are eighteen epilepsy charities in the UK. Each one of them would, if it could, run a national advertising campaign telling the public that it alone services and represents the interests of people with epilepsy. Charities provide the raw materials, estimates of the incidence of the impairment in society, their list of 'good works', their hopes of expansion, and so on, but the ad agency is very much the tail that wagged the dog. It sets its own brief. This three-stage corporate process is the ideal of the agency. However, the relationships that different impairment charities have with different 'giving' ad agencies are extremely varied. And any systematic advertising programme is liable to fall at the first gust of adversity. A regular scenario is that an agency might devise the three stages of the campaign without informing the charity (who in turn is too frightened to ask) of the cost of placing the ads in the media and on national billboards. These placings of the advertising in turn may be arbitrary and opportunistic; often they will depend on media space buyers within the agency getting reductions for their charity proofs from late cancellations. Clearly, one of the problems of this relationship is this stop-go effect that it has on the public positioning of the work.

That aside, the first stage is to create 'brand awareness' imagery which visualises the impairment and very subtly links it to the charity client. It attempts to create a photographic image which will aid the public to 'see' what is to a large degree socially invisible and hidden through segregation. (The impairment may also be apparently hidden itself, like epilepsy, cancer or diabetes.) The task for the agency is to find an image which gives the impairment and its effects a symbolic but social identity. Since the impairment has to be the site of disablement, it follows that the body of the person with an impairment will be constructed as both the essence and symbol of disablement. Their body becomes fragmented and refocuses on the major fragment – the impairment. The object of this first stage, then, is to place the symbol of the impairment into a social orbit but labelled as the property or concern of the affixed charity. This is branding.

A portrait will be put together within a minimal social environment ('neither dead nor alive, neither out of society nor wholly in it') and this image will appear simply to reflect 'society's' neglect of this impaired person. The main body of text in this first image or image-series will then context the image. It tells the viewer how to read the image and it will appear to be an account of existing with the impairment. Critically, the text may interrupt the retrogressive image and appear to challenge it. That is to say, the photograph is despairing and it has manufactured fear or dread or pity in the viewer; the text shows that help is possible; where that help will come from is written in small, meek, modest text at the foot of the page – the charity's name. What's in a name? Well, quite a lot; this impairment charity has a corporate identity and a hegemony to establish. At this first stage, the charity is unlikely to put an address by its name. It probably won't have a PO box for income. It will calmly and simply exist. Remember your Sunday school? Goodness is good, goodness is simple, goodness doesn't shout from the rooftops!

The central purpose of this stage is not to fix the impairment (nor even income needs) to the mast of the charity too blatantly; it is primarily to fix the existence of the impairment in the mind of the public. This designer-modesty exists to instil the notion that the charity is not in fact making claims for itself at all. The campaign may be occupying a million pounds' worth of free More O'Ferrall advertising sites[13] but each poster must appear to fuse the concern of a doctor with the divinity of a nun. It denies that it is in fact marketing itself at all. It is merely making claims on behalf of 'its' disabled group (that is, its type of impairment).

The denial by the charity that is in the business of marketing its wares is a key element if it is to be publicly accepted as an object of voluntary giving. However, the point of this 'branding' first stage is, in reality, to do just that. The designer-humility is an important tactic since this advertising is in fact competing not just with the other 170,000-odd charities but also with the entire gambit of commercial advertising. It has to exist in this jungle but appear to desist from the fight. In this, all impairment charities have used a number of common devices to demonstrate a genre which is different from commercial advertising. However, like all advertising, charity advertising needs both similarities and distinguishing marks. One common feature of charity advertising is that it is almost always in black and white, while commercial advertising is almost entirely in colour. Charity advertising sells fear, while commercial advertising sells desire. While you binge on luxuries, remember the dispossessed. Cripples are contaminated waste, but the experts are handling it. Charities promote a brand not to buy, but to buy your distance from. In a sense then, charity advertising hunts in packs within a similar terrain of soliciting giving.

Crucially, in any critical reading of charity advertising, the first stage or tenet sets up a continuum which exists throughout *all* charity advertising. This continuum is what might be called *the double bind*. This is to say that the charity carries at least two separately located meanings (one in the photograph, one in the text) which are autonomous but consumed as one. On the one hand, the photograph shows dependency and, if taken in isolation, futility and oblivion. The text to this image/person, however, might have a 'scientific' challenge to the pictorial oblivion by adding objective 'facts' about the impairment. This is the double bind. It is a double bind because both meanings are read almost at once and appear unified within the 'piece of mind' of the consumer. Their meanings are, however, quite different and often opposing but have the purpose of setting up the *dependent impairment–active charity* dynamic in your head. The image posits futility and hopelessness, while the text suggests methods of cure, care or eradication. There is the past but there is a future. The simplicity of the logo of the charity at the bottom tells you who will make the future.

In the second stage of charity advertising, which might be known as attitude change, the 'piece of mind' is consolidated. Again, the same double bind of oppressive image versus textual hope is again mobilised but appears to have progressed. In this second stage of the campaign, the assumption is that the public are now interested and that the condition can be elaborated upon. This, however, will take the form of a description of the charity's efforts to alleviate or cure the impairment, not how the disabled person is organising against his or her oppression. It is within this explanation of the impairment, and how to cure or care for it, that the corporatism of the impairment equals charity equation will be stepped up and consolidated.

'Attitude change' is the charities' dream of social change without political action. It leaves the mechanics of oppression intact on the body, while it pioneers new methods of identity and representational oppression. In other words, 'attitude change' as used in charity advertising asks disabled and non-disabled people to disengage from the physical world of inaccessible construction and enter a mapless world of hope. It will only be a short move before the boomerang of 'attitude change' returns to those who are the centre of this whole discourse, namely disabled people. Which disabled person has not been told to make more of an effort? Which disabled person has not been told to try harder? Which disabled people has not been told that they 'have a negative attitude'?

While all the fight at all stages is for a piece of mind, at this stage the fight is to activate the viewer within their consciousness but not yet within their purse. The purpose of the charity promoting 'attitude change' is to harness the notion that the charity is fighting for different attitudes to disabled people. What happens in this second stage of the charity establishing its corporate identity is a tightening of the double bind of charity imagery, in which again the essential tragedy and passivity of disablement is shown in the impairment or 'flaw' but against which is set text which appears to elaborate and challenge it. Imagery showing the progress of the flaw or impairment will appear as the second frame in a slow, uncertain movie which began in the first stage. This progression may be downward or it may be sideways, but it will not be upwards in terms of the impairment character flaw. If in the attitude change, second-stage imagery the character appears to be enriched, it is only because of the riches of the charity.

This process can be seen in any number of campaigns. The Multiple Sclerosis Society's first stage was the establishment of the tear, the rip as the branding of both the impairment and the society. The second stage, which they have just begun, shows a series of posters including a 30-year-old man being bathed and a ballet dancer dancing to a mortality timer (Plate 3). The first stage had beautiful people living in nothing but their destroyed beauty. Like Greek demi-gods, they had no purpose other than to be beautiful, and then they lost that. The beast had come upon them. In the second stage, the man-in-the-bath poster is constructed as being symbolic of the despair of the MS decline. This is the progress between stages one and two. MS has thus been turned into a symbolic condition, rather than an actual one. In this sense, the MS is no longer real but is designed to mirror a fictional manifestation of the fear within the viewer. He has a mothering figure of a woman bathe his physical self and his symbolic soul. The image shows his broad back with her large hands and her muscular arms across it. Her sleeves are rolled up, she has a job to do. Her head leans forward and her forehead almost connects with his. Her activity and his passivity are constructed as the sexual nightmare of all (heterosexual) men. Despite his bulky torso, he does not fill the bath. His body is in the middle. He has been infantilised by his condition. His head tips down and this apparent sadness is written in the text, which reads, 'How does it feel to have a mental age of thirty and a physical age of one?' The final twist in this sorry saga is the apparent awfulness of knowing that his mind is trapped in an asexual infantilised body.

The shift in text within the stage-two charity advertising is crucial. Whereas in the first stage, text was minimal and objective (that is, impairment specific), the text in stage two either comments and illuminates the condition, or appears to quote the 'sufferer', or challenges the viewer's reading of the negative photograph. That is, the text takes an involved position on the impairment: it unites both the charity and the giver's gaze on the impairment. It is engaged in the agenda and it has moved on from merely noting the existence of the impairment (and the charity). The name and address of the charity may, in many instances, be even smaller in this series of ads, so absolute is their confidence at being read as the custodians of the rights to the solution of their brand of impairment. So, the first stage introduced us to the objective horror of 'MS'. This was consolidated in the tying of MS to the Multiple Sclerosis Society in the second stage of images, which show the metaphysical downward progress of the impairment. The text in the second stage develops a position on the impairment, a view of its progress and the implications, not just a registering of its existence. The text is the unified voice of both the charity and the viewer. The stretching away of the passive image from the active text posits the charity as a possible solution. Without them, it suggests, there is no hope. The *photography* itself is hopeless.

Again, a Spastics Society image of cerebral palsy shows a bed located in an institution with an air tent and oxygen tank surrounding it, while the main text reads: 'Could this be where I got my Spirit of Adventure and my Love for Camping?' (see Plate 1). The photograph clearly demonstrates disablement within the care/cure of the institutions. It is categorically depicted as a medical issue. The text shows the acquiescence in this view by the subject, the person with cerebral palsy, and thus infers the acquiescence of all people with cerebral palsy to the notion of the medical view of impairment as disability, charity as solution. This poster is quite an advanced attitude-change image because it has used the voice of a disabled person to bend the charity's and the viewer's gaze on the disabled person. The problem for many people decoding these adverts is that the double bind brings together two sets of messages, that of the photograph and that of the text, which appear contradictory. A double take then happens in which the viewer reads first the negative image and then corrects himself or herself (not necessarily consciously) with the text. This internal dialogue by the viewer is crucial to an acceptance these images as representing reality. The voice-over by the person with the charity's particular impairment also locates the impairment, again, with the charity.

So, having shown the world first that the charity represents the interests of particular impaired people who cannot self-function (branding) and second, that the charity is going to do something about this intolerable state (attitude change), the charities use the third stage, which shows the ongoing servicing provided by the charity of their impaired people. This latter stage might be called the functional stage. Images in this section are characterised by photographs of disabled people being metaphorically carried out of their body-centric impairment oblivion and beginning to function, but only with the aid of tools provided by the charity through donations. This has strong links with attitude change but the difference is that the disabled person is beginning to engage in functional space. The Spastics Society ran a series of posters showing disabled people using services which they had developed. The services (and images) ranged from adapted spoons to feed people with cerebral palsy to images of three men moving into a bungalow. It appears that this stage of photography is starting to approach something like the social model of disablement, but again the double bind image/text relationship comes into play within the development of these 'functionalist' images' relation to the text.

Thus the photographs in this stage appear to begin to show the disabled person in some form of social engagement. To counterbalance this, and to protect the impairment charities' hegemony through corporate identification of themselves with the impairment, these adverts switch the job which the image originally performed. This is a key development. The text is now expected to play the more 'negative' role of locating the exercise within the charity. It combines both the descriptive and personal elements of phase two to show that the functional efforts of the disabled people portrayed are financially dependent on the charity. Within the Spastics Society's poster showing a photograph of three men at the door of a bungalow (they have just moved away from a residential unit), the text quotes them as saying, 'Today we live in a home of our own. It took us about a year to move, and of course we needed a bit of help from our friends at the Spastics Society. To be honest, we still do.' Clearly, the double bind of image-text positioning is still intact. The impairment is still the site of the issue, it is still a flaw. The functionalist movement of the disabled people portrayed is that of ventriloquist's dummy manipulated by charity. Their ability to function socially is dependent on voluntary giving as well as charitable distribution. The impairment cannot be overcome but it can almost be circumvented. However, it must still be foregrounded in the poster as the currency of the charity. It is their produce. The impairment-as-flaw is still so conspicuously constructed that the apparent slight progressiveness of the text takes on more of a wish than a reality. The disabled person symbolically comes close to entering the charity-giver dialogue, but is met with a 'Yes dear, here's a pound' collusion between the viewer and the charity.

The charities are beginning to create these 'users of the services' third-stage functionalist images for two main reasons. First, as was previously outlined, there is strong pressure both externally and internally for charities to market their services and to replace declining state provision, particularly within the 'Care in the Community' context. Second, the pressure on charities and their advertising from the disability movement is becoming more and more difficult to withstand. The Telethon 1990 demonstrations made plain the conflict between the charity advertising representation of disablement (as the lost body or part of the body of the disabled person) and the growing presence of a political body of disabled people seeking access and rights. The impairment charities simply cannot ignore the fact that those whom they ask society to see as their own ranks, the handicapped, are disabled people in revolt. So this third stage is to a large extent a rearguard amalgamation of these forces. It is also the point at which the charities specifically seek voluntary giving and name the purpose of this income as the fuel for the activitation of the person or impairment portrayed. However, as charities give ground to the arguments of the disability civil rights movement, and as the disability movement develops image-processes of its own, I have no doubt the charities will attempt to develop a fourth-stage, 'positive' image of their impairment category both to show how happy their users are and to fight off criticism. It cannot be overemphasised, however, that these changes are likely to continue to locate disablement in the body or on the subject of impairment, not in social oppression. This may be seen within much of the vogue of word changing, whereby 'handicap' is out of fashion in the charities, likewise 'disabled person', but paradoxically *person with a disability* is 'in'. Needless to say, the UK disability movement is clear that 'disabled people' is the only term that should be used and it has rejected this wordgame-as-solution to social inaccessibility and misrepresentation. Rejection of these side-issues brings out the wounded-child look from grown adults within charities when told that their special formula for the solution of disablement, to call 'them' 'people with disabilities' still locates disablement on the person and is thus an obscuring rather than an illuminating process. Will retitling black people as 'people with black skin' shift capitalist imperialism and domestic racism? Perhaps they should develop a 'fourth-stage' advertising campaign for internal and external consumption, promoting disabled people to the key points of the organisation's power. Somehow I doubt this will happen.

I am describing a triple-stage 'model' of charity advertising which is drawn from the sum of the parts of a wide range of impairment charity advertising. It describes a process from which much, if not most, impairment advertising stems. However, I would not wish to suggest that all charities are consciously pursuing this path. To make such an assumption would give impairment charities far more credit and power than they deserve. What the three stages within the mechanics of impairment charity advertising demonstrate is the basic consensus of approach among the charities towards both disablement and advertising. In handing over the visual construction and representation of 'their impairment' to the ad agencies, the charities demonstrate their real sensibilities (as opposed to those professed by the adverts) towards the people they seek to represent. It is as if the Labour Party were to set up an advertising campaign and call it 'Scroungers!' Furthermore, charity advertising is by no means systematic. It can be very erratic and subject to a whole host of internal problems, including the fact that the charities themselves are often the most oblivious to the effects and purpose of their advertising (though this is not an excuse).

The point I am making by outlining these three stages is to show the process that is common to many charities who wish to position themselves through advertising. It is likely that this trend will continue to grow. The notion of a *process* of charity image making is also important to grasp (and this I return to in Chapter 7) because some people are being seduced into seeing the different stages as a 'positive' move on from the previous one. All charity advertising, in the final analysis, must somewhere in its poster posit the notion of its particular brand of impairment being dependent on charity. It is ridiculous to ask anything else of impairment charities.

But going back to the charities themselves (rather than the work of their ad agencies), there is a considerable amount of trepidation around this triple-stage graduated placing of the charity/impairment in the public mind. This resistance is based not on any issues of morality about oppressive imagery (except perhaps from the one or two executive members who have the impairment) but on the common myth of how charity advertising works which pervades so many charity management boards. This myth is that posters go up on the hoardings with a coupon telling the givers where to send their donations and the money comes rolling in. This myth was described to me by a charity member as the 'think of a number and double it' wish. That is, if you spend x on a poster, you will automatically get double-x in return. This is in fact the opposite of the truth, but charity people time and time again told me how they had believed this simple equation and so faced the consequences.

> We ran a campaign last year and the primary purpose was to raise money. We wanted people to relate the activity which we were showing them in the posters to the money that they would be giving. We felt it would give them a sense of purpose in their giving. . . . The fact of the matter is that while the advertisements overall were subsidised and did not cost us a lot of money, the actual money recouped was barely 15 per cent of our outlay. The campaign expenditure was £20,000 and it brought in £3,000.[14]

And again from another charity:

> I remember one advertising campaign we ran. We had posters on 600 underground sites in London which ran for a month. That's 18,000 days of advertising.

We did use the standard monitoring device of putting a PO box on the ads so we could see how people were responding. I think we got one cheque, for a £100, from a man whose mother used to give to us.[15]

Charities themselves became the victims of their own myths and propaganda. The central myth is that they exist exclusively in a two-way flow of giving between themselves and the public. However, their total income is broken down between assets, trading, and voluntary giving. Of the voluntary giving, around a third represents giving by legacy. The other two-thirds of voluntary income, comes from a host of sources including covenanted giving, payroll giving and the income generated by the volunteers. However, charity advertising publicly marshals this diversity of income into the one single myth of voluntary giving. It is imperative for both the charities' fiscal privileges and their social status in society, as well as their apparent domination of the disability agenda, that they are not seen to be active in business (or in politics). They portray themselves as the innocents of the commercial world, passively waiting for goodness to translate into income. Advertising is often viewed as the declaration of their goodness equalling an avalanche of financial admirers.

Take the Multiple Sclerosis Society. Their Tears Lives Apart rip has become the symbol by which they and multiple sclerosis have become branded, that is, connected together in the public consciousness. The campaign which depicted the body beautiful being ripped by the scourge of multiple sclerosis is known colloquially by the ad agency who dreamt it up as 'Beauty and the Beast'.[16] Even the most superficial analysis of these adverts would suggest that the MS Society depends for its operations on the public responding specifically to them by giving money. However, an analysis of the income of the MS Society reveals that their total voluntary income for the year 1987/8 (Year Two of the Tear campaign) was £6,546,000; of which £4,654,000 was from legacies and 'other gifts' and the rest (£1,572,000) from voluntary fund raising.[17] This 'voluntary fund raising' itself was probably broken down to include jumble sales, tea-parties, whist drives, flag-day collections and so on. During the years of the Tear campaign, the MS Society has fallen from 32 (1987) to 38 (1989) in the league table of fund-raising charities. What is more, this fall in their voluntary income from £6,886,000 (1988) suggests that the 'negative' Tear campaign could be losing the MS Society up to a third of a million pounds per year![18] Furthermore, the research quoted below suggests that the income generated by charity advertising, including the MS ad campaigns, which have a national profile and have made MS (to quote the ad agency) 'second or third in the league of nasties', may in fact be minuscule compared to the overall voluntary income. Even with a high-profile 3-stage campaign, it is clear that the MS Society have not gained the voluntary income results they would have hoped for.

While it is surprising that charity advertising and public giving do not have the simple relationship they are assumed to have, this fact is nevertheless privately admitted by many of the charities and confirmed in some public research, in particular, the recent report by the Charities Aid Foundation entitled *Charity Household Survey 1989/90: Who Gives What . . . and Why?*[19] Under point *2.2.2, Prompted Giving*, the survey analysed ways in which the public give to charity. They listed methods of prompted giving (responding to an appeal of some sort), including door-to-door, street collections, pub and shop counter collections, collections at work, sponsoring someone in an event, responding to an appeal advertisement, responding to a mailshot, and so on. They found that the commonest method was responding to door-to-door collections and that *one of the least used methods of prompted giving was responding to advertising appeals. Indeed, only 1 per cent were found to respond to this method!*

Reading the findings of this report, and using my own research, a more accurate picture of the process of income generation by charities, and the role of advertising within this scheme, begins to emerge. It is becoming clear (and I suspect to the charities, though their research on this is considered a commercial secret) that the central point of charity advertising is not in the first instance to raise money: at this it manifestly fails. Its central purpose is to appeal to the volunteer army of the respective charity organised within regional and local 'self-help' groups. Charity advertising is there to inform these people that they exist and that their mission is happening. As one executive member of the 'brand leader' charity in its field told me:

When this agency boss wanted to help our charity – his wife had the condition – we thought, great, an end to our problems. It was done free and we thought, fine. Well, they produced a poster which went all over the country and which everyone on the executive agreed, with hindsight, was financially useless. You had a nice bleak picture. White background, red borders, they didn't even use our colours. At the top, it showed a girl staring out at you, and above in big, bold, black text were the words, 'She Doesn't Have Cancer, She Hasn't Been Abused, But She Needs Your Help'.

   Now, I have to say that we all very much regret letting this ad out, but it did go out and it was all around the country. Anyway, at the bottom in small type was our name and a PO box to send your donations to, blah, blah. It was a direct appeal for cash. Nationally, I think it brought in under £100. But what it did do, despite how terrible we at HQ thought it was, was to tell the members out there that we were doing something, that they were doing something. The members saw it and wrote in with, 'At last, something from my association!' It didn't matter what was on the ad, you could've put that, people with —— are a load of rabbit f——! It wouldn't have mattered.[20]

The advertising imagery showing hordes of half-life dysfunctionals isolated by their impairment and their charity, takes no account of either the subjective feelings of those with the impairment – the 'victims' – or of those of us who organise not along impairment lines but along disablement lines, but they most certainly do take account of their volunteers. The statistic of giving by house-to-house collection was the highest percentage of all the seventeen methods which the CAF researchers put to people (32 per cent), with the third highest percentage being street collection (24 per cent). It is from within these massed ranks of volunteers that the psychology and philosophy of charity advertising is dispersed in *real terms*. The advertising works along the lines of commercial 'negative advertising' in that it consolidates a position but doesn't create it. For instance, 'negative' car advertising may be telling people not so much to buy a particular car but that the car they have already bought is the best one.

The real effect of 'negative' advertising for the charity, in terms of response and income, depends quite critically on the number of volunteers in the field doing the gathering through the more effective methods. The point of advertising, and this is why ad agencies push their charity clients to accept a three-tier gradual approach, is to create a corporate relationship between the impairment and the charity which speaks a credible story to a public, but which the membership can also feel validated by. The fear that charity advertising promotes in its images of particular impairments is itself contained by the possibility of a catharsis by the viewer on to the charity advert. Thus the social fear of loss of labour-power (within regulated production), narcissism or of mortality appears contained. The point of national campaigns is that then and only then is the membership able to mobilise income once the doorstep giver has registered the impairment-fear/charity-salvation equation from the particular advertising. The advertising has entered the public domain and has set an agenda inside the potential givers. However, to tap this source, the charity most certainly needs a large volunteer army. Again, to quote a 'brand-leading' charity:

> Every year this corporate thing comes up at the executive. Each year, when we announce yet another shortfall of £200,000, someone says, well, er, I think, you know, it's because we don't do well on flag-days. They think, if only our flags were a different colour! It's not because we've only got twenty people on the streets of London, as opposed to 2,000 which some of the larger charities have, and it's not because nobody knows we exist, it's because our flags are the wrong colour![21]

However, large-scale advertising plus a large collecting army does not alone explain why people give to particular charities. How do the images of fear operate in the first place? The research in this area is sparse and has only been conducted publicly in the UK by the Charities Aid Foundation. As I explained earlier in Chapter 3, the extent of actual giving is greatly exaggerated within the media. Furthermore, there are signs that giving per household is decreasing and that it is 'highly unlikely that there has been any real increase in individual charitable giving over the period 1987–90'.[22] This downward pressure on charities may impel them to carry out more thorough investigations (and consequently result in more substantial publications) into exactly why people give.

But for now, a pattern is emerging from my research into the question: Why give at all? The central reason for giving to, and volunteering for, a particular charity is the psychic or social presence of the condition or impairment within the living or folk memory of the giver. This is to say, people give to charities representing the impairments which they have personally experienced on a primary or secondary level. The CAF found that, of those who had considered giving to charity in their will (legacy giving), 43 per cent would leave money to a charity which was particularly relevant to their life – such as a charity to fight cancer or heart disease if that had affected them.[23] Of the total respondents to their survey, including those who had not considered giving to charity at all, 14 per cent also agreed with this sentiment. Furthermore, a survey of charity giving in wills or legacies revealed that people giving in the generally poorer area of Yorkshire gave more often to charity than those in the more prosperous south-east. The study by Smee & Ford and IFM Consulting showed that nearly one in six wills in Halifax contained a bequest to charity. While this survey did not specifically analyse impairment charities, it does demonstrate a correlation between givers and their experience of the condition.[24] Clearly, giving to and prioritising charities bear a correlation to the presence of the impairment or condition within givers' localities, families or communities. Disappointingly, the CAF failed to ask people in the section on 'Volunteering' if they gave their time as a result of a personal or familial affinity or experience of the impairment. But it is here that a picture (or spectre) of the charity image *raison d'être* emerged. In my interviews the occurrence of people with the impairment within the charity or ad agency was significant, though still representing a small minority of the total employees; it was most definitely not prevalent in the seats of power within the organisation. Nevertheless, the issue of charity-based disabled people's (albeit minority) support for oppressive impairment imagery does need to be addressed.

Many of these isolated disabled people had internalised the notion that disablement was indeed located on or in the impaired body, otherwise they would not have organised through charity. For them, save more of the same, there is nowhere to expand to within this position and within a charity organised along impairment lines. Many were on a futile chase, caught up in a fury and anger which they couldn't quite name, a silent raging anger at the isolation of their condition. Since the social construction of disablement had not been dealt with on any level within the charity or the local 'self-help' group (except where hinted at within 'attitude change' campaigns which, as we have seen, confirmed more than they challenged), the people with the impairment appeared to have nowhere to give vent to this rage. That disabled people operating in charities were, in fact, within one of the key sites of struggle – the impairment charities – was to think the unthinkable.

Many disabled people have lived their entire lives with notions of their worthlessness, adhering to the belief that their very life-force depended on professionals and superiors. It is not suprising that some disabled people very easily acquiesced in other people's vision of them. The imagery produced by the charity is produced at the top and appears to speak to individual disabled people within the charity, and to their isolation. People with the impairment within the charity come in on a yes/no basis to these images but have no real control over the making of the image. The image and the process are presented as facts. And indeed the advertising appears as a fact: disabled people are oppressed, the image is oppressive, it seems thus to be telling the story of their oppression, not contributing to it. The fact that the image is in itself oppressive *of them* often appears incidental, it merely confirms the futility of their rage and their position. Their agreement in 'supporting' this impossible double-bind state of affairs is given, if it is given, because the imagery appears at least to make their private anger public.

For the disabled people within the impairment charities, grouped at the 'self-help' bottom of the hierarchy, and hoping that their non-disabled 'superiors' will produce solutions to them as a 'problem', their confirmation and even support for the negative imagery is a final nihilistic statement within the politics of despair, for they have accepted the definition of impairment as flaw. Also, while impairment charity advertising may be portraying the social death of disabled people, it does not actually show corpses. (The 'dead dog' advertising abandoned by the RSPCA has never quite entered impairment charity advertising.) The absence of the portrayal of actual death (which would rob the viewer of any glimmer of hope and therefore any purpose for the charity) may seem like a bonus to some isolated disabled people. That is, they may see that the imagery *does not* exactly show the process of social death which the segregation of disabled people into 'special-needs' institutions is designed to facilitate. There is no doubt that many disabled people who work through the charities are older and have spent more time within segregated institutions. They have had longer to be oppressed by their apparent valuelessness: much of their life may have been that of the institutionalised living dead since the purpose of phase-two institutions is to suspend the 'socially dead' until their actual physical deaths.[25] Therefore, *any hint of any existence at all within the social domain is considered 'positive'*, even if it treats them like a commodity owned by a charity and voyeuristically exposes their bodies to the impersonal gaze of the masses: the image appears to bear a resemblance to a survivor! When there appears to be only one route to validation and to a social currency for disabled people, and this route is the charity image, and when the life of being buried within phase-two worthlessness has been ignored and silenced, it is suprising that more disabled people do not validate charity advertising. That they do not is testimony to the ability of many disabled people to locate their oppression and fight it, not to validate notions of stigma and the tragic flaw. No blame can be attached to those disabled people who see possibilities in charity advertising. It is the lack of alternative representational references which leads to a certain fixation for some with this form.

To this image creation and consumption process is added the non-disabled psyche. I was very surprised by the extent to which the social condition of the impairment was within the life-experience of the people who worked on the advertising (both within the ad companies and the charities). There were ad agency creative directors who personally had the impairment (but very much not out). There were account directors whose grandmothers had died of the condition. There were even charity executive members who supported other charities because their friends, their best man, their sister-in-law and others 'had it'. And every one of them viewed this 'having it' as an act of martyrdom; tragic but brave. Not one of them expressed to me a political questioning of the isolation that this or that member of their extended family or community experienced. Phase-two notions had indeed become 'common sense'.

Surely it is here that the very heart of charity imagery is born. The non-disabled controlling interest in charities' organisation, and the non-disabled givers, both remember (perhaps guiltily, perhaps painfully) their own local or personal version of the impairment. They also see the current version of the impairment within their own family, community or charity. The hegemony of the millions of charity posters block out a different view of disablement and repeatedly confirm the impairment as disability. This blaming of the victim appears to be officially sanctioned by organisations that 'support' disability, and the non-disabled public who may not see that the charity advertising itself has constructed the hyperdependency of disablement. It is as if the public are viewing their past guilt in the physical presence of the impairment image. This is compounded by the internalised rage and futility which they have begun to view as a physical attribute of the impairment. Even the clearly political demonstrations against charity appeals, or for accessible transport or integrated education, are construed as the rage of the disabled soul against the impaired 'flaw'.

Isolation and loss, then, is how the consumer is taught to characterise the impairment. They hope that the image will prove cathartic both for themselves and for the disabled people they organise or give to and will heal the memory or presence within their own lives. It cannot, because it is expected to heal the social disablement and social death in which impaired people are expected to exist, and which the charity itself plays a vital part in propagating. Charity advertising speaks to the part of non-disabled people who must, within the extended family or the community, have a folk or personal memory of life with an impairment. They remember the impairment, they see the charity image. This appears to have externalised the memory or the pain. Perhaps, they feel, giving will purge the memory forever. Regardless of the co-ordinated campaigns of advertising, direct mail, co-ordinated press work, volunteer door-to-door and street collecting which most charities aspire to, these activities will not sustain a voluntary income unless this personal connection is made by the giver.

The pain, isolation or guilt of the giver through this connection is quite real. Their experience of disablement, whether first or second hand, is necessarily within 'phase two'. The systematic segregation of disabled people away from a work-based system and into a needs-based system is within the collective memory and is here and now. There is no anti-discrimination legislation establishing civil rights for disabled people in the UK. The issue also may be compounded by the separateness of disabled people born not into groups of primary identification, such as class, colour or gender, but into primary isolation within the family as well as within community and society. It is not difficult to see how the impairment can become the target for multiple levels of displacement and disavowal experienced by people of their implication within the disabling process and also how this can lead to a despair for the possibility of change. (It goes without saying that the disability movement is fighting these notions. Also, I don't doubt for one moment that many non-disabled people are also struggling against these oppressive conditions and genuinely pursue the path of access and rights.)

Charity advertising is both the parasite which lives off this confusion and the public ordination of it. It represents the highest public validation of the isolation of disabled people. It presents a solution to the 'problem' of disablement by a disguised blaming of the victim. It fails to find a solution because it is itself the problem. But what is missing from charity advertising is the centre of this grand solution – the separating out of the impairment from the disablement, the medical view from the social view. The dominant form of impairment imagery, that of charity advertising, cannot demonstrate this struggle because the very essence of charities is to obstruct the making of this link.

Charity advertising ultimately fails not only because it cannot acknowledge, let alone solve, the issue of social disablement (although it cannot), not because it doesn't directly generate enough money (although it doesn't), and not because the impairment is not the disability (although it isn't). It fails because it is the visual flagship for the myth of the tragedy of impairment. It is the higher ground to which all non-disabled society looks to unburden its guilt and its 'able-bodied' anxiety. What constructs itself as the heart of a heartless nation is itself one of the great bastions of oppression of disabled people. The real 'tragic flaw' of this form of disability representation is the existence of the impairment charity itself.

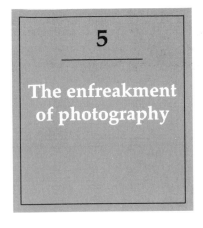

5

The enfreakment of photography

Before reading this chapter, I feel I must contextualise what lies ahead for the reader. In many ways, charity advertising as oppressive imagery appears to be the *bête noire* of disabled people. Unfortunately, oppressive as it is, it represents colours of a social order tied to a specific mast. Those colours and constructions also exist in other areas of photographic representation. This is demonstrated in this chapter. I ask the reader to join me on a journey into oppressive disability imagery. At times, particularly in the examination of the work of Diane Arbus, it can be depressing. However this chapter is here because I feel we have to take the fight against constructed oppression (whether by non-access or by representation) into the camp of the oppressors.

Apart from charity advertising, when did you last see a picture of a disabled person? It almost certainly wasn't in commercial advertising since disabled people are not thought to constitute a body of consumers and therefore do not generally warrant inclusion. It might have been within an 'in-house' health service magazine, in which disabled people are positioned to enflesh the theories of their oppressors. The stories might range from the successes of a toxic drugs company to the latest body armour for people with cerebral palsy, and some person with the proverbial 'disease' will be shown illustrating the solution and its usefulness. It might have been in an educational magazine, in which a non-disabled 'facilitator' will regale in words and text the latest prototype 'image-workshop', using disabled people as guinea pigs while developing their 'educational' ideas. The text brags about the colonisation of disabled people's bodies and identities, while the images show how much 'the disabled' enjoyed it. Passive and stiff and 'done to', the images bear a bizarre resemblance to colonial pictures where 'the blacks' stand frozen and curious, while 'whitey' lounges confident and sure. Whitey knows the purpose of the image, the black people appear not to (or at least, perhaps as employees, have no right to record visual dissent).

The 'positive' side of their ultra-minority inclusion, then, is that disabled people are there to demonstrate the successes of their administrators.[1] Apart from the above areas, however, disabled people are almost entirely absent from photographic genres or discussion because they are read as socially dead and as not having a role to play. But although the absence is near absolute, the non-representation of disabled people is not quite total. Taking the structured absence as given, I wanted to discover the terms on which disabled people *were* admitted into photographic representation. As Mary Daly once wrote of feminism, the job entails being a full-time, low-paid researcher of your own destiny.[2]

I visited one of the largest photographic bookshops in London and leafed through the publications. Generally disabled people were absent, but there was a sort of presence. Disabled people are represented but almost exclusively as symbols of 'otherness' placed within equations which have no engagement to them and which take their non-integration as a natural by-product of their impairment.

I picked books at random. *The Family of Man*; *Another Way of Telling*; *diane arbus*; *Figments from the Real World*. There were obviously lateral associations but only one, *diane arbus*, I knew to include images of disabled people. In the research for this book, I had begun to uncover sometimes hidden, sometimes open, but always continuous constructions of disabled people as outsiders admitted into culture as symbols of fear or pity. This was particularly true in literature[3] but I wanted to see if it held true in photography, so I picked the books at random. They may have been connected in styles or schools but, as far as I knew, had no connection whatsoever on disability representation. Only Arbus was infamous for having centred disabled people in her work but I felt an uneasy faith that all of them would 'use' disabled people somewhere.

The first book examined was entitled *The Family of Man*.[4] The Family of Man exhibition at the National Museum of Modern Art, New York, in 1955 is considered the seminal exhibition for humanist-realist photography. It was the photographic height of postwar idealism. It showed the great 'positive image' of an unproblematised and noble world – a world from which pain was banished. Where there are images of 'working folk', their muscles and their sweat appear to be a part of the great spiritual order of things. Where there are images of black people, the images show poverty; some show harmony, but all are visually poetic. Black life has been harmonised through aesthetics.

However, throughout the catalogue of the show, which contained 503 images shot from 68 countries by 273 male and female photographers, there is only one photograph of someone identifiably disabled. This is more than an oversight. Put together ten years after the Second World War, *The Family of Man* was about 'positively' forgetting the past and all its misery. Forward into glory, backward into pain! Although this publication and exhibition heralded a brave new world of postwar hope and harmony, on reading it it becomes clear that the inclusion of disabled people – even disabled people tidied up like black people and working people – was not a part of the postwar visual nirvana. Why was this?

The one image of a disabled person appears on the penultimate page of the 192-page publication. It is mixed in among six other images on that page and is part of the final section of the book, which covers children. Children are shown laughing, playing, dancing, crying and so on. Of the thirty-eight images in this section, three buck this trend. The three are all on this penultimate page. In the final section, after five pages of innocent joy, you encounter on the sixth page three that remind you it is not like that always. At the top of these three is a disabled boy who appears to be a below-the-knee amputee. He is racing along the beach with a crutch under his right arm. He is playing and chasing a football. His body tilts to our right as he approaches the ball, while his crutch tilts to our left, to form a shape like an open and upright compass. The ball is situated in the triangle which his left leg and his right-side crutch make on the sand. The triangle shape is completed by a shadow which the boy casts from his right leg to the crutch (and beyond). The ball enters this triangle focusing point but his right leg does not. Its absence is accentuated and impairment here is read as loss. The game he plays is his personal effort to overcome his loss.

The photograph creates a flowing but awkward symmetry and our reading of its flow is continually interrupted by the fact that the triangle's neatness is dependent on the absence of a limb. Two readings occur simultaneously: it is tragic but he is brave. In a book of hope, the disabled person is the symbol of loss. The disabled boy is a reminder that all is not necessarily well in the world but *he* is doing *his* best to sort it out. The image is 'positive' in that he is 'positively' adjusting to his loss. Because he is 'positively' adjusting to his loss, the image is allowed into the exhibition and the catalogue. The image of his disablement has been used not for him but against him. The image's symbolic value is that disability is an issue for the person with an impairment, not an issue for a world being (inaccessibly) reconstructed. In *The Family of Man*, disabled people were almost entirely absented because harmony was seen to rest in the full operation of an idealised working body. The exhibition and catalogue did not admit disabled people (bar one) because it did not see a position for disabled people within the new model army of postwar production or consumption.

Photographically speaking, the decline of this high ground of postwar hope in the 'one world, one voice, one leader' humanity was heralded (in historical photographic terms) by an equally influential but far more subversive exhibition, again at the Museum of Modern Art, New York, which was held in 1967. This exhibition was called New Documents and brought into a wide public consciousness reportage portraiture showing the human race as an alienated species bewildered by its existence. New Documents featured the work of Gary Winogrand, Lee Friedlander and Diane Arbus. The importance of these three photographers (and others like Robert Frank) is that their work heralded the breakdown of the universal humanism of *The Family of Man* into a more fragmented, psychic or surrealistic realism. The appalling reverse of the coin is that they anchored the new forms of a fragmented universe (to a greater or lesser extent) in new, even more oppressive images of disabled people.

What is particularly crucial in terms of the representation of disabled people in this photojournalism is a clear (yet still uncritical) emergence of the portrayal of disabled people as the *symbol* of this new (dis)order. Whereas the tucked-away disabled person in *The Family of Man* had been a hidden blemish on the body of humanity, in a world of the Cold War, the Cuban Missile Crisis and Vietnam, disabled people were represented as the inconcealable birthmark of fear and chaos. Diane Arbus was the second photographer whose work I looked at. The monograph that I had pulled from the shelf is from her posthumous retrospective, held at the Museum of Modern Art, New York, in 1972 and entitled *diane arbus*.[5]

Of all photographers who have included or excluded disabled people, Diane Arbus is the most notorious. She was born into an *arriviste* family of immigrants, whose money was made in the fur trade. She became a photographer through her husband, Allan Arbus, and worked with him in fashion photography. She moved away from that (and him) into work which still dealt with the body and its surrounding hyperbole but from a very different angle. It was on her own and in her own work that she became known, unwittingly according to her, as 'the photographer of freaks'. Whether she liked it or not, there can be no doubt that this is how her work has been received. The monograph contains 81 black-and-white images, of which eleven are of disabled people. These eleven can be divided into three quite critical periods of her work. The first is demonstrated in two portraits of 'dwarfs'; the second with the portrait of the 'Jewish giant'; and the third with the imagery shot just before her death, that of the 'retardees' (her term for people with Down's Syndrome).

In any of the material on Arbus, including this monograph, Patricia Bosworth's biography of her entitled *Diane Arbus, A Biography*, and Susan Sontag's discussion of her work in *On Photography*, the stages of her oppressive representations of disabled people are never discussed. Moreover, the 'factual' recording of disabled people as freaks is accepted totally without question by major critics like Sontag, who says, 'Her work shows people who are pathetic, pitiable, as well as repulsive, but it does not arouse any compassionate feelings.'[6] Later, she rhetorically adds, 'Do they see themselves, the viewer wonders, like *that*? Do they know how grotesque they are?' (her italics). Sontag brings to the disability imagery of Arbus a complete faith in Arbus's images as unproblematic truth-tellers. Bosworth also colludes by patronising disabled people, telling us of Arbus's 'gentle and patient' way with 'them'. Neither of these critics, it goes without saying, considered asking the observed what *they* felt about the images in which they figured. Once again, the entire discourse has absented the voice of those at its centre – disabled people.

Since there is only one other book on Arbus's work, and that deals with her magazine work,[7] it is safe to say that Bosworth and Sontag represent key parts of the Arbus industry. In their validations of Arbus's work, they both miss a central point. Although she was profoundly misguided (as I demonstrate further on), there can be no doubt that her work paradoxically had the effect of problematising, or opening up, the issue of the representation of disabled people. Her critics and defenders have built a wall around her work (and any discussion of disability in her work) by 'naturalising' the content. In this, the images of disabled people have been lumped into one label, that of 'freaks'. Perhaps this has been done because her work appears to buck the contradictory trend of 'compassion' in the portrayal of disabled 'victims' practised by other photographers. Although Arbus's work can never be 'reclaimed', it has to be noted that her work, and the use of 'enfreakment' as message and metaphor, is far more complicated than either her defenders or critics acknowledge. The process of analysis is not to rehabilitate her or her work but to break it down once and for all.

She was a part of the 'snapshot aesthetic' which grew up beyond the New Documents exhibition and exhibitors. This form attempted to overturn the sophisticated and high-technique processes of the Hollywood fantasy portrait, as well as rejecting the beautiful toning of much of *The Family of Man*. However, more than any of her peers, she took this aesthetic nearer to its roots in the family photograph or album (indeed she intended to shoot a project entitled Family Album).[8] Arbus had experienced, in her own family, the emotional and psychological cost of wealth in terms of the painful subjectivity and isolation of the individual hidden and silenced within the outward signs of bourgeois upward mobility and success. In terms of disability, however, Arbus read the bodily impairment of her disabled subject as a sign of disorder, even chaos; that is, as a physical manifestation of *her* chaos, *her* horror. Despite her relationships with disabled people (often lasting a decade or more) she viewed these not as social and equal relationships but as encounters with souls from an underworld.

There was nothing new in this pattern of 'reading' the visual site of a disabled person away from a personal value into a symbolic value which then seals the representational fate of the disabled person. However, at least in the first period of her disability work, Arbus deviated from the Richard III syndrome by reading this 'disorder' as the manifestation of a psychic disorder not in the subject but in society. There is no question of Arbus using her subjects 'positively' – it is clear that she always intended them and their relationships to themselves and others to symbolise something other than themselves. She saw herself and her 'freaks' as fellow travellers into a living oblivion, a social death. There is a perverse sense in which she was right – disabled people are expected to inhabit a living death – but the crucial thing is that she considered her projection to be more important than their reality. She 'normalised' subjects like Morales, *The Mexican Dwarf*,[9] or *The Russian Midget Friends*[10] by specifically placing them in that great site of bourgeois culture and consumption, the home. The 'horror' of Arbus's work is not that she has created Frankenstein but that she moved him in next door! What is more, the freak had brought his family! The 'shock' for the hundreds of thousands of non-disabled viewers was that these portraits revealed a hinterland existing in spite of the segregationist non-disabled world view.

For Arbus, the family – her own family – represented an abyss. She saw in the bourgeois promise to the immigrant family, her own family, a Faustian contract. Her Mephistopheles, her threat to the bourgeois privilege, was to move a non-disabled fear that dare not speak its name into the family snap. In a sense, this first period of her work (a period not of time but of understanding) is her least oppressive and in some ways complete. The sitters acknowledge her presence and her camera. They stare out from the picture at the viewer. Far from making apologies for their presence, they are distinctly proud, they are committed to their identity. Although the disabled people portrayed existed within subcultures (such as the circus), they were clearly not segregated and it is this which shocked the public who flocked to her posthumous retrospective at the Museum of Modern Art in 1972. It is the *conscious dialogue* between Arbus and the subjects which 'horrified' and yet fascinated people more used to compassionate victim images of disabled people obligingly subhuman and oligingly institutionalised as 'tragic but brave'. Morales, the Mexican 'dwarf' in *diane arbus*, is pictured naked but for a towel over his crutch. He wears a trilby at a rakish angle and his elbow leans casually on to the sideboard, resting just in front of a bottle of liquor. It is not clear quite what went on between Arbus and Morales (though Arbus had previously 'spent the night' with another disabled subject, Moondance, as part of his agreement to be photographed) but the eroticism of the image cannot be denied. Not only is the so-called 'dwarf' distinctly unfreaky in his three-quarters nakedness, he is positively virile! A constant theme of Arbus's work, not just of her disability work, is the relationship between people's bodies and their paraphernalia. While the attire is crisp and clear, the flesh of the subject has been 'zombified'. This, however, is not the case with her first pictures of 'dwarfs'. Morales's body is very much alive.

Arbus had attempted to trace the psychic disorder of consumer society back to a primal state of terror within everyday life. That she believed disabled people to be the visual witness of this primal state is clear. That is, she accepted at the level of 'common sense' the non-integration of disabled people. However, much of 'the Horror, the Horror'[11] with which Arbus's work has been received is in her location of this disabled terror within non-disabled normality. The disabled subjects themselves, at least in this early 'freak' work, are treated reverentially. The camera is close. The camera is engaged. The subject has agreed to the session (but agreed in isolation?). The 'horror' of the process for non-disabled society is in her placing a disabled normality within a non-disabled normality. The horror is in how she could even think them equivalent. The horror, I repeat, was in Arbus's recording in her constructions of disabled people a double bind of segregation/non-segregation. The 'non-segregation', however (and this is where Arbus's crime really lay) did not lead towards integration – the 'Russian midgets' were not living down the road as part of an independent living scheme – but towards transgression. It was a spectacle, not a political dialectic (the disability paradox) that Arbus wanted to ensnare. For this she accepted, indeed depended, on the given segregation of disabled people as 'common sense'.

Things begin to disintegrate for Arbus in the second part of her disability work. This is illustrated in the monograph by the image entitled *A Jewish Giant at Home with his Parents in the Bronx, N.Y. 1970*. Again, we see a cosy family setting of a front room with two comfy chairs and a sofa, two elderly and self-respecting pensioners, a lamp by the drawn curtains, a reproduction classic painting in a tasteful frame, and a giant. The 'giant' is not given a name in the title but his name was Eddie Carmel.[12] Again, Arbus did not sneak in and sneak out in this shot but got to know and photograph Eddie Carmel over a period of ten years before printing this one which she considered to work. This image of *A Jewish Giant* with its glaring flash-lit room, its portrayal of 'the beast' from the womb of the mother, shows less harmony, even a deliberate asymmetry from that of her 'dwarf' images. In *A Jewish Giant* she had created an image which took her beyond the reverence in both form and content of her 'dwarf' images. Unlike them, Eddie the Jewish 'giant' directs his attention away from the presence of the camera, his only acknowledgement that an image is being made is by being on his feet like his parents. His body language appears unclear and unsettled. The flash has cast black halos round the bodies of the subjects and they begin to resemble a Weegee as a found specimen of urban horror. The image of the 'giant' as he crouches towards his more formal parents is that of a father over two children. The classic family portrait of parents and child is completely reversed by her use of their size relationship. The body language of the 'Jewish giant' is more 'out of control' (that is, it diverges more from non-disabled body language signs) than that of the 'dwarfs'. It is all the more 'threatening' to the non-disabled family snap because his body is situated with that of his 'normal' parents. A clash or a confrontation between styles and discourses is occurring. The alchemy, confrontation and visual disorder of the image bring Arbus closer to avenging the control and repression in her own family. This is the key to her use and manipulation of isolated disabled people. During the ten years of their knowing each other, Eddie Carmel told Arbus about his ambitions, about his job selling insurance, about his acting hopes (and his despair at only being offered 'monster' roles), and so on. Arbus dismissed this in her representations. She clearly found his actual day-by-day life irrelevant. Indeed, she appears to have disbelieved him, preferring her own projection of a metaphysical decline. His real tragedy is that he trusted Arbus, and she abused that trust outside of their relationship in an area within her total control, that is, photography.

The visual dialogue within the image between herself and the subject in the 'dwarf' works, although decreasing in the imagery of Eddie the 'giant', was still prevalent and was important precisely because it created a snapshot family album currency within the imagery. The commonness of this form was a part of its communicative power. As a structure it spoke to millions, while its content, Arbus's enfreakment of disabled people,[13] spoke to the able-bodied fear of millions. Were the subject to disengage, to reject the apparent co-conspiracy (in reality a coercion) or contract between themselves and Arbus, the images would move from the genre of family album currency and understanding of millions, to a reportage subgenre position of one specialist photographer. Arbus's work would then be that of an outsider constructing outsiders which need not be internalised by the viewer. The enfreakment in her disability images was internalised by the non-disabled viewers because the disabled subjects, while chosen for their apparent difference, manifested body language and identity traits recognisable to everyone. Arbus was concerned to show the dichotomy, even the pain, between how people projected themselves and how she thought they 'really' were. The projection of this 'imagined self' by the subject was through the direct gaze to camera (and therefore direct gaze to viewer). The image of *A Jewish Giant*, to Arbus, suggested a higher level of fear and chaos than the 'dwarf' work. This higher level of discrepancy between order (the setting is still the family at home) and chaos (Eddie outgrowing that which contained him), than that manifested in the 'dwarf' work, is also highlighted by the fact that, although the 'giant' is on his feet posing with his parents, his dialogue is as much between him and his parents as between him and Arbus/the viewer.

Arbus was reported to have told a journalist at the *New Yorker* of her excitement over this image, the first one that had worked for her in the ten years of photographing Eddie. 'You know how every mother has nightmares when she's pregnant that her baby will be born a monster? I think I got that in the mother's face as she glares up at Eddie, thinking, "OH MY GOD, NO!" '[14] You could be forgiven for imagining that the mother recoils from her Eddie much like Fay Ray recoiled from the horror of King Kong, but this is not the case. Arbus betrayed in her excited phone call to the journalist what she wished the image to say, rather than what it actually does say (though, of course, meanings shift). Arbus's comment about 'every mother's nightmare' speaks of her nightmare relationship with her own body, which I believe she viewed as the sole site of her power. It was this loss of control of the body which she saw disability/impairment as meaning. Arbus once quoted a person who defined horror as the relationship between sex and death. She also claimed that she never refused a person who asked her to sleep with them. Furthermore, Bosworth hints that Arbus may have been confused about her bi-sexuality. In any event, the clues suggest that while she viewed her body and sexuality as key points of her power, her sexuality was not clear to her, and sex itself probably failed to resolve her feelings of aloneness and fragmentation. She sought the answer to this dilemma in locating bodily chaos in all her subjects (to varying degrees) and felt she'd found it in its perfect form in disabled people. (That major institutions of American representation, like the Museum of Modern Art, promoted her work shows their willingness to co-operate with this oppressive construction of disabled people.)

The 'OH MY GOD, NO!' which she attributes to the mother in *A Jewish Giant* is in reality an 'OH MY GOD, YES!' victory call that Arbus herself felt. She had made her psychic vision physical, or so she felt. Diane Arbus's daughter, Doon Arbus, has written that her mother wanted to photograph not what was evil but what was *forbidden*.[15] She believed she had pictured a return of the forbidden and repressed within her own remembered family. In her construction, the awkwardness of *A Jewish Giant* hints at the unwieldiness of her vision as a long-term solution to her own needs and begins to hint at this vision's ultimate destructiveness – not only, and obviously, to disabled people, but to the psychic well-being of Arbus herself.

It is here that the third period in her work on disabled people begins. She starts to photograph 'retardees' (as she labels people with Down's Syndrome). She moves from observing her subjects at home to observing them in a home; that is, an institution. These images of people with Down's Syndrome were practically the last she shot before killing herself. They are clustered, six of them, at the end of the book. In her previous work with 'dwarfs' and *A Jewish Giant* Arbus had maintained that she did not photograph anybody who did not agree to be photographed. This was undoubtedly so (although coercion is probably truer than agreement), but the images show a decline in the conscious frontal participation of the subject. This decline was also mirrored in the growing discordance on the technical side of her work. The beautiful tones of Morales, the 'dwarf', give way to a harsh flash-light in the 'Jewish giant'. There is no doubt that Arbus, as an ex-fashion photographer, knew what she was doing in using technical disharmony as an underwriting of the narrative disharmony. When we come into the third period, her work on 'retardees', Arbus continues to pursue technical discordance. She still uses flash-and-daylight to pick up the figures from their landscape, but the focus is clearly weaker than that of the previous work. The subjects are now barely engaged with Arbus/the viewer *as themselves*. Arbus finds them not in a position to conspire with her projection. The visual dialogue collapses. The dialectic between body and attire which Arbus had pursued is broken. The chaos of their paper and blanket costumes appears, to her, not to challenge their bodies but to match them. Arbus's order–chaos paradoxical projection has not happened. Instead, Arbus sees zombies in another world. To her they project no illusions of being neighbours to normality. These people are not at home but in a home. The institution of the family gives way to the institution of segregation (in this case, a New Jersey 'home' for 'retardees'). The people with Down's Syndrome are set in a backdrop of large open fields showing only distant woods. For Arbus, their consciousness and activity is arbitrary. She does not know how to make them perform to her psycho-ventriloquist needs. In her career-long attempt to pull the psychic underworld into the physical overworld by manipulating the bodies of disabled people, she has come to the borders in these images. She had met 'the limits of her imagination'; she had not found in these images the catharsis necessary for her to continue. Arbus first loved then hated this last work. She entered a crisis of identity because these segregated people with Down's Syndrome would not perform as an echo of her despair. Because of this, her despair deepened. In the final image of this series and the final image of the monograph, nine disabled people pass across the view of the camera. Of the nine, only one turns towards the camera. His gaze misses the camera; consequently the possibilities that might have been opened up by a direct gaze are, for Arbus, lost. He joins the rest of this crowd who come into the frame for no purpose and leave the frame with no purpose. Arbus's camera became irrelevant not only for disabled people, but for Arbus herself. This was her last work before she killed herself.

The next book I looked at was Gary Winogrand's *Figments from the Real World*.[16] Of the 179 black-and-white plates in *Figments from the Real World*, six included the portrayal of disabled people on one level or another. Like Arbus, the inclusion of disabled people, regardless of their role, was that of a significant minority with their oppression unquestioned and constructed as intact. Unlike Arbus's work, however, Winogrand did not produce any images (at least not for public consumption) whose central character was the disabled person or disablement. He did produce bodies of work on women, for example, but where a disabled person appears in the work, it is as a secondary character to the women. Nevertheless, within the 'under-representation' in *Figments from the Real World*, it becomes clear that, like Arbus and the others from my ersatz list, 'the disabled' had a role to play. Nevertheless, Winogrand consciously or otherwise included disabled people with the specific intention of enfreaking disability in order to make available to his visual repertoire a key *destabilising* factor.

With regard to the representation of women by Winogrand, Victor Burgin has critiqued Winogrand's work and has explored the reading of meaning within his imagery and the relationship of this meaning to the wider social and political discourses of his time.[17] Burgin describes and discusses an image of Winogrand from an exhibition in 1976. The image is of four women advancing towards the camera down a city street. The group of women, who are varying degrees of middle age, is the most prominent feature in the right-hand half of the image; equally prominent is a group of huge plastic bags stuffed full of garbage. The introduction to the catalogue of the exhibition makes it clear that this 'joke' is intended. The reading of middle-aged women as 'old bags' is unavoidable.

Despite the protestations by John Szarkowski in the introduction of *Figments from the Real World* that Winogrand celebrated women (he called the book of this phase of his work, *Women are Beautiful*), it is clear that his construction of women singly or in groups advancing towards the camera from all directions displays an unease, a fear, of what the results of his desire for them might be. Their faces frown by his camera, their eyes bow down to avoid his gaze. Burgin highlighted the dynamics of his 'old bag' image. Winogrand's fear at what he reads as a loss of (female) beauty in ageing is registered by his 'old bag' image. It is no coincidence that one of the six disability images (and the only one of two showing a wheelchair user) in *Figments from the Real World* involves an almost identical dynamic to that of the 'old bags'.

The centre of the image is three young women. They are lit by a sun behind them and their sharp shadows converge towards the camera. They dominate the centre third of the image and they are walking along a ray of light towards the lens. They are dressed in the fashion of the moment. In their movement is recorded an affecting, perhaps transitional beauty. Their symmetry is, however, broken by the gaze of the woman on the right. The symmetry is further challenged by this woman being a step ahead of the other two as she stares down at the presence, in the shadows, of a crouched wheelchair user. The other two women slightly move their heads towards the wheelchair. All of their eyes are tightened and all of their facial expressions 'interpret' the presence of the wheelchair user with degrees of controlled horror.

Unlike Winogrand's dumping of middle-aged women into 'old bags', he confronts these young women with a warning. He observes them as beautiful but warns them that their beauty and all its 'paraphernalia' is all that separates them from the 'grotesque' form they are witnessing. Beauty is warned of the beast. Clearly, Winogrand could not assuage his desire for women, whom he spent years photographically accosting on the street. His work harbours a resentment that they do not respond to his aggressive desire and so he implants warnings. The asymmetry of the imagery is anchored in the non-disabled reading (in this instant, Winogrand's) of disabled people as sites of asymmetrical disharmony. The women's body harmony (as Winogrand desires it) is set against the wheelchair user's disharmony (as Winogrand sees it). Winogrand's use of the disabled person, again enfreaked, is to bring out of the underworld and into the shadows a symbol of asymmetry *as fear and decay* which challenges the three women's right to walk 'beautifully' down the street.

Like Arbus, Winogrand's use of disability is to warn the 'normal' world that their assumptions are fragile. This he does by the use of the differentness of many disabled people's bodies as a symbol of the profound asymmetry of consumer society, particularly in the United States. Despite the fact that the American President Roosevelt had been disabled, the enfreakment of disabled people in these new practices became the symbol of the alienation of humanity which these new photographers were trying to record.

The Family of Man exhibition had all but excluded disabled people because they did not represent hope in the new order, so the post New Documents practitioners *included* disabled people for precisely the same reasons. The Family of Man and the New Documents exhibitions, constructed within photographic theories as radically separate, are inextricably linked, in that the inclusion of disabled people does not mean progress, but regression. Disabled people increased their presence in the new reportage of these photographers not as a sign of enlightenment and integration, but as a sign of bedlam.

The fourth book picked at random, I realised afterwards, takes us to a European setting. In *Another Way of Telling*,[18] the inevitable inclusion of a disabled subject comes almost at the very beginning. The book deals heavily with photographs of the countryside and the peasantry of various countries and the first photo-text piece sets this agenda. This is a story of Jean Mohr taking photographs of some cows, while the cow owner jokingly chastises him for taking pictures without permission and without payment. This first part very much sets the geographic and political agenda for the whole book, which explores the three-way relationship between the photographer, the photographed and the different meanings and readings taken from the photographs.

In every image or image-sequence, excluding the second one in the book (that of a blind girl in India) the images are more or less openly problematical. That is, the relationship between the image and its apparent informative or communicative value is put to the test. 'Only occasionally is an image self-sufficient,' says Jean Mohr. From this assertion, Mohr and Berger explore the image-making processes and what can be taken on or used within the process of photography that might work for both the photographer and the subject. The genesis of the book is to question meaning and use-value of imagery from all points, not just that of the photographer.

In Mohr's eighty-page first part, he illuminates different contexts of his own image-making, from shooting running children from a passing train, to shooting and re-shooting working people and directing his work according to their expressed wishes. The theme which pervades the whole book is that of the working process. Moreover, the working process that they have chosen to explore visually is that of people working on the land and their lives and communities. The image-sequences, whether of cow-herders or of wood-cutters, begin with labour and its dignity. Clearly, unlike many 'concerned' social realist photographers, Mohr is attempting to inhabit the process from the inside, not just to observe it externally. His method is through the voice, feedback and acknowledgement of the person photographed in their work. Their work is the anchor, the base, from which the story unfolds.

At one point and in one sequence, Mohr turns the camera on himself. He puts himself in the picture. He talks about the fear, the anxiety, even the panic which assails many people when they are the subject of the camera. Am I too fat? Am I too skinny? Is my nose too large? He tells us that he finds the process of putting himself in the picture difficult and talks about how he attempts to lose his image through technical disguises, like deliberately moving the camera during an exposure so as to blur the image, and so on. He anchors this process of putting himself in the picture on the quite valid and narcissistic idea that he used to imagine that he looked like Samuel Beckett. After bringing the story home by saying that he was finally forced to view his own image by being the subject matter of *other* people's lens, rather than his own, he finally finishes it by telling us that a student who photographed him felt that he did indeed resemble Beckett.

His work on other people's images and stories and his work on his own image and self are linked because, in grappling with the process of representation of his self or of others, he tells us and attempts to show us that the meaning of images is rooted in the process and context in which they were made. This is an important assertion but not unique. This book was published in 1982 and came at a time when other photographers and theorists, like Victor Burgin, Allan Sekula, Photography Workshop (Jo Spence/Terry Dennett) *et al.*, were questioning and problematising the naturalist truth-telling assumptions underpinning the left's use of social realist photography. *Another Way of Telling*, then, was a part of this 'movement'.

However, *Another Way of Telling*, and Jean Mohr's opening piece in particular, is clearly anchored in finding another way of using naturalist reportage, not abandoning it altogether. Mohr explores the use-value of the naturalist image to the subject. He tells stories of how this or that peasant wanted the image to show the whole body – of the person, of the cow, of the tree-cutting process – rather than be 'unnaturally' cropped. Naturalism, then, to him, has a purpose *in context*.

Here, we begin to get close to the *purpose* of the blind girl pictures within Jean Mohr's piece and the book as a whole. The realist (time/place) agenda is set in the first image, that of the cowman, but the *underlying agenda of 'simple' naturalism* (that is to say, Mohr and Berger's belief in its ability to tell a simple story) is anchored in the hypersimplicity of the blind girl's pleasure. These pictures of a disabled person – a blind Asian girl – form the apex of the book's naturalist thesis that the value of naturalism is in its portrayal of unconscious innocence.

The story is called 'The Stranger who Imitated Animals'. The 'stranger' in question is Jean Mohr. In the 250-odd words which accompany the five images, he tells us of visiting his sister in the university town of Aligarh in India and of his sister's 'warning' of the blind girl who comes round and likes to know what is happening. He awakes the next morning unclear of where he is when

The young blind girl said Good Morning. The sun had been up for hours. Without reasoning why I replied to her by yapping like a dog. Her face froze for a moment. Then I imitated a cat caterwauling. And the expression on her face behind the netting changed to one of recognition and complicity in my play-acting. I went on to a peacock's cry, a horse whinnying, a large animal growling – like a circus. With each act and according to our mood, her expression changed. Her face was so beautiful that, without stopping our game, I picked up my camera and took some pictures of her. She will never see these photographs. For her I shall simply remain the invisible stranger who imitated animals.[19]

Clearly, despite his simplification of his response ('without reasoning why'), he responded with impersonations precisely because he had observed that she was blind. He objectified her, his first impulse on waking up to see a blind person was to play games with the blindness. Underlying this was the assumption that blind people (whatever the level of visual impairment) have no idea of quantifiable physical reality and would, of course, think that the sound really was of a yapping dog waking up in bed. His joke reveals his disability (un-) consciousness, not hers.

But she responds to this with laughter, she joins in. So, he further objectifies her by again distancing himself. While she laughs along with his imitations, he secretly photographs her, because her laughing but blind face was 'so beautiful'. Clearly, because she is laughing in his pictures, he presumably continued his imitations while he photographed her. The game for two turned into manipulation by one. The pictures show her leaning against the dark wooden surround of the door. She is framed by this and leans into this frame by pressing her ears to his mimicry. She is kept at a distance and keeps her responses on that surface of the mosquito net which fits into the wooden frame. This framing of her by the door is copied in his framing of her in the camera. Out of the five pictures in the sequence, four clearly show her eyes. Technically, these have been deliberately whitened in the printing to highlight the blindness.

As labour is the anchor in the other series, and as narcissism is the anchor in his self-image series, shooting the whites of her eyes is the anchor in this series. Her blindness is the symbol of innocence and nobility. Her blindness is the anchor of her simplicity. Her blindness is the object of his voyeurism. He has taken and symbolised this disabled person's image, which he says 'she will never see' (he obviously didn't consider aural description), as the anchor and beauty of naturalism. The text which accompanies this series of images doesn't quite have the once-upon-a-time-ness of some of the other photo-essays, but it still serves to push the imagery into the magical or metaphysical. The always-to-be natural images of the blind girl are the only set that have no significant time element to them. His work with the cowman spans days, his work with the wood-cutter is over a period of time (enough for the wood-cutter to give an opinion of the finished prints), but the work with the blind girl of beauty and innocence needs saying once, because it is forever. Again, like *The Family of Man*, like Arbus and Winogrand, Mohr has chosen to absent both the three-dimensional disabled person and their social story because it is incongruous to their own disability (un)consciousness. Their images tell us nothing about the actual lives of disabled people, but they add to the history of oppressive representation.

I have just analysed a random selection of four major photographic books, only one of which I knew to have been involved in disability representation. In the event, all four were. In the final analysis, these books which include disabled people in their field of photographic reference do so on the condition that disabled people are, to use Sontag's term for Diane Arbus's work, 'borderline' cases. Sontag meant this term in its common reference to psychic or spiritual disorder. However, disabled people in the representations which I have discussed in this and the previous chapters share a commonality in that they live in different camps beyond the border. Whether beauty or the beast, they are outsiders. The basis for this border in society is real. It is physical and it is called segregation. The social absence of disabled people creates a vacuum in which the visual meanings attributable (symbolically, metaphorically, psychically, etc.) to impairment and disablement appear free-floating and devoid of an actual people. In the absence of disabled people, the meaning in the disabled person and their body is made by those who survey. They attempt to shift the disablement on to the impairment, and the impairment into a flaw. The very absence of disabled people in positions of power and representation deepens the use of this 'flaw' in their images. The repression of disabled people makes it more likely that the symbolic use of disablement by non-disabled people is a sinister or mythologist one. Disablement re-enters the social world through photographic representation, but in the re-entry its meaning is tied not by the observed, disabled people, but by the non-disabled observers.

It is here that all the work, picked at random, is linked. Disabled people, in these photographic representations, are positioned either as meaningful or meaningless bodies. They are meaningful only as polarised anchors of naturalist humility or psychic terror. Brave but tragic: two sides of the segregated coin? Disabled people are taken into the themes pursued by Arbus, Winogrand, Mohr, and so on, to illustrate the truth of their respective grand narratives. The role of the body of the disabled person is to enflesh the thesis or theme of the photographer's work, despite the fact that most of the photographers had taken no conscious decision to work 'on' disability. It is as if the spirit of the photographer's mission can be summed up in their manipulation of a disabled person's image. 'The disabled' emerge, like a lost tribe, to fulfil a role for these photographers but not for themselves.

Disabled people appeared either as one image at a time per book or one role per book. The use of disabled people is the anchor of the weird, that is, the fear within. They are used as the symbol of enfreakment or the surrealism of all society. 'Reactionary' users of this notion hunt the 'crips' down to validate chaos within their own environment (Arbus); 'progressive' users of this notion hunt them down within their own environment to find an essential romantic humanity in their own lives (but no question of access). The US 'crip' symbol denotes alienation. The impaired body is the site and symbol of all alienation. It is psychic alienation made physical. The 'contorted' body is the final process and statement of a painful mind.

While this symbol functions as a 'property' of disabled people as viewed by these photographers, it does not function as *the* property of those disabled people observed. Its purpose was not as a role model, or as references for observed people, but as the voyeuristic property of the non-disabled gaze. Moreover, the impairment of the disabled person became the mark, the target for a disavowal, a ridding, of the existential fears and fantasies of non-disabled people. This 'symbolic' use of disablement knows no classic political lines, indeed it may be said to become more oppressive the further left you move.[20] The point is clear. If the disability paradox, the disability dialectic, is between impaired people and disabling social conditions, then the photographers we have just examined represent the construction of an 'official' history of blame from the disabling society towards disabled people.

The works were selected at random and I fear their randomness proves my point. Wherever I drilled, I would have found the same substance. Were I to continue through modern photographic publications, I have no doubt that the pattern I am describing would continue; the only variation being that some would use disabled people for the purposes described, while others would absent disabled people altogether. A cursory widening of the list, to glance at photographers who have come after those named above, people like Joel-Peter Witkin,[21] Gene Lambert,[22] Bernard F. Stehle,[23] Nicholas Nixon,[24] and others who have all 'dealt with' disablement, shows photographers who continued a manipulation of the disability/impairment image but have done so in a manner which depressingly makes the work by, say, Arbus and Mohr (I don't suppose they ever felt they'd be mentioned in the same breath!) seem positively timid! The work of many of the 'post New Documentaries' has shifted the ground on the representation of disabled people by making 'them' an even more separate category. While the volume of representation is higher, the categorisation, control and manipulation have become deeper. In this sense, the photographic observation of disablement has increasingly become the art of categorisation and surveillance. Also, from a psychological viewpoint, those that appear to have transgressed this commodification of disabled people have only transgressed their own fears of their constructions. The oppression remains the same. The segregated are not being integrated, they are being broken into! The photographic construction of disabled people continues through the use of disabled people in imagery as the site of fear, loss or pity. Those who are prevented by their liberal instincts from 'coming out' in their cripple-as-freak, freak-as-warning-of-chaos, circumvent it by attempting to tell the unreconstructed 'natural' story of oblivion. Either way, it is a no-win victim position for disabled people within those forms of representation. My intention in this book is to suggest new forms.

A final note of hope. Diane Arbus was 'extremely upset' when she received a reply from 'The Little People's Convention' to her request to photograph them. They wrote that, 'We have our own little person to photograph us.'[25] In terms of disabled people's empowerment, this is the single most important statement in all of the work considered. It is my intention that the next chapter takes disability image-making further into the self-affirming camp of disabled people and their allies.

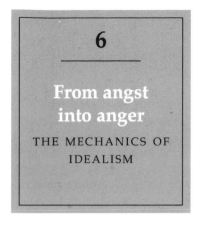

I first became a photographer when I was 19. More correctly, I became an entrepreneur who used a camera and a squirrel monkey to make money. I was a 'smudger'. This was the nickname given to seafront photographers who daily shot hundreds of holiday snaps for the holidaying punters who would pay, with degrees of coercion, various prices for various 'packs' or combinations of the same image. We used very small Olympus Pen-E half-frame cameras, which meant that we could shoot seventy-two portraits, and log the details of the punter into the accompanying address and purchase slips, before having to get the boss to change the film for us. The format of centring the punters in front of a recognisable landmark with the sun on our backs was never altered. If they appeared particularly gullible, we might shoot a second and third picture, the portrait shot, or the action shot, in order to increase the sales. The photography was entirely incidental as far as I was concerned. The art of the job was not photography, it was selling. Smudging was a serious profession with serious money to be made. Yarmouth, Southend, Blackpool, Scarborough, Brighton, Wembley market, all the areas were covered by smudgers; I worked most of them.

Each year, the smudging bosses would vote for their resort's Smudger of the Year. My sister Christine won Smudger of the Year in Yarmouth for sticking to her pitch in all hours and all weathers and building up trade based on small but consistent sales. The Smudgers' Ball would be held in one of those function suites which had carpet on the walls and which became the mark of working-class affluent leisure in the mid-1970s. Like parody capitalists with their fat cigars and fat bellies, the smudging bosses would sit together at the 'high table' and lie through their teeth about their profits. We would regale each other with hilarious stories of the past season. There would invariably be a fight.

I loved it, and I hated it. During my seasons as a smudger, I was also a fine art painting degree student. More correctly, I was a fine art degree student who spent the Easter and summers and some Christmases 'smudging'. That both forms, the high art and the low art, ran concurrently seemed to me at the time to be a curse. I wanted to be a fine artist and I saw myself as merely 'passing through' the smudging before I fully occupied a place in 'Art'. The term was vague and had no real meaning to me, although I attempted to enflesh it with modernist theory *à la* Clement Greenberg, which I then balanced up by writing an atrocious and pretentious final-year dissertation entitled 'Art as visual ideology: the history of Marxist aesthetics'.

The contradictions abounded. I worked on the seafront as a smudger although I studied in the citadel as an artist. I was from a working-class family but I wanted, with aristocratic simplicity, *to paint*. I split into personalities to which I attached moral stabilisers. If this part wanted to paint, it must study socialist art theory. If that part was a moneymaker, the evenings must be spent reading Proust. I realise now that the dialectical fragmentation was a necessary breaking up and a growing up. I also realise that what I wanted was choice but I saw choices as absolute positions which had to be kept apart. The period of undergraduate study eventually turned out to be an intense photographic training. One form I overvalued and the other I undervalued.

One part of me, however, my epilepsy, was buried deeply beneath all of this surface transformation. It was a pain and a wound which had no 'dialectical' opposite. A fear that dare not speak its name, it was the site of sheer terror. I hated it, I cursed it, but it stuck to me like a birthmark. Epilepsy was untransformable, it could not be parodied or reinvented. It knew no guises when it came out and, beyond the piercing four-day headache and depression, it appeared to leave no mark when it left. All the other personality creations pressed ahead away from it. My Marxist self, my artistic self, my wide-boy self were Spartans defending the bridge to this Valley of the Dead. I really saw nothing in epilepsy and disablement but hell.

I left college and went to London. Thatcherism was growing and the value of people was decreasing. What did internal chaos matter when there were political battles to fight? While the left got stuck in, there was no room for the subjective. As if feminism had never happened, 'Ditch the Bitch' became a socialist anti-Thatcher slogan. It was ditched itself, when the single-identity male order of the left was itself challenged by a 'post-modernist' alliance of fragmented and reclaimed identities from the black sections, women, lesbians and gays, disabled people and so on, who saw the white, male 'norm' itself as a site of struggle and oppression. Many of these new groupings in turn ditched notions of class not only as a political category but as a social category altogether. Those who reclaimed their identities in turn silenced others. I myself felt once again split. I was from a working-class family but the materialist idealists of the new identities were telling me that class, my life, had never happened. On the other hand, the brutal materialists, from the Stalinists to the Labour Party 'right-wingers', saw the answer to capitalism and identity as one of correct management and denied any subjectivity whatsoever. Subjectivity was something you did when you were drunk, and regretted the next day.

I was attempting to build a castle on shifting sands. Political parties, ideological schools, wings and genres all spoke to parts of me. I would try and funnel the other parts through each isolated part. I could never quite manage it. Most parts of me, the post-study working class, the second-generation Irish, the artist, the Marxist, the feminist man (the disabled person was still deeply buried and inadmissible) could be cobbled together superficially and made to make sense in particular circles at particular times. The performance appeared real, even persuasive, but a hunted animal that is wounded has no time to deal with the wound. I tried to adopt the 'objective' route to self-change, which was supposed to happen through abstract notions of social change and education. It was interesting to be around people, mostly men, who attempted to control their lives and their destinies through impersonal politics. While I hid the black hole of epilepsy and disablement within my self I tried to join them. Most of the political people I met during this time were not strangers to pain. They too were the walking wounded. It's just that the last place they could go to either personally or politically was within themselves. We knew more about Third World politics than we knew about our own livers. Despite feminism, I found that within male-dominated politics, the personal was still inadmissible.

I can remember the day when I gave up the silence. I came out to a 'comrade' that I was an epileptic. He lowered his paper, looked at me, and said, 'I had a friend who was an epileptic. He drank too much and died on a train.' Shocked by this, I said in fear, 'Did he die of a seizure?' 'That's irrelevant', he replied. 'The incontrovertible fact is that he is dead.' He then changed the subject to the future of Eastern Europe.

It became clear to me that the feminist claim that 'objectivity' is really male subjectivity was true. A therapeutic reading of the comrade's utterances might suggest that he wanted epilepsy, and my voicing it, to be dead. The problem was that perhaps I did too. Each time I 'came out', similar responses of silencing occurred. I was in a double bind because, although I was filled with a chaotic rage when they pushed my coming out back down my throat, I felt myself capitulate to their silencing of myself as a disabled person because I too wished 'it' were dead and silent. Despite the attempts and the guises, I was brought back, once again, to my great unpronounceable fear that dare not speak its name. Once again, I had tried to reinvent most parts of myself but I could not reinvent the burning core of my self, the epilepsy and disablement. It was time to meet the dread. I found and joined the disability movement. The journey into the valley had ended and the journey out of the valley begun.

The switch from advocate to shaman is an important one. Although abstract political theory (that is, the 'left') was inhabited by many of 'the walking wounded', the fact that they never named their pain has, I feel, created a dialectic between themselves constructed as 'objective' and those in whose name they struggled, who were moved into the victim position as 'subjective'. Like Miranda from *The Tempest*, they suffered with those they saw suffer.[1] Miranda stood on dry ground observing a shipwreck. I gave up the Miranda syndrome and admitted my own wreckage. I had viewed epilepsy as the worst junk in my psychic and physical scrapyard but an evangelical conversion which I described in the introduction came into being. Of course, the impairment did not alter. I was not cured. Indeed, I abandoned the notion of cure. The 'passing' was supposed to confer on me a privileged disabled person status. If I named my impairment, the threat (surprisingly consistent and communal) was the withdrawal of my 'right' to pass. I learnt quickly that I was being asked to conduct a half-life. The social living death of disabled people had become 'phase-two' common sense. Did I really want it to be like that? I realised that the hidden power contract was to stay like 'us' or be obliterated.

As if the world were suddenly put to rights, a number of things started to come together. As a photographer working within the disability movement, I came upon a number of discourses which had reached either breaking point or fruition. The movement for access was up and running. Disabled people were coming out of the institutions and day centres in anger at their conditions. People were coming out of physical or psychic prisons into a powerful personal and political light. For many, there was literally nothing to lose, and whereas in other struggles a hundred would vote to strike and six would turn up for picket duty, everyone who went for action came on the day. The energy is and was extraordinary. Of course, what I and others were bearing witness to was the living political transformation of the medical model of disablement into the social model of disablement. It was this magic and transformation that I began to photograph. As I had found a form within myself which was in harmony, so I began to develop a form of photographic representation which I felt might reflect the harmony of myself and of others within the disability movement.

There is a lesson I learnt when I started out as a photographer. I spent some time assisting a photographer who regularly worked for a high-profile business magazine. He worked on a 4″ × 5″ camera and took time, through Polaroids, to form the body language of the sitters into important, direct power poses. The subjects were 'captains of industry' who used their bodies to carry their brains around. The fact that many of those photographed were, in reality, disintegrating, vastly overweight and tucking their shirts into their underpants was all hidden by the designs of the photographer's images which stripped down the subject into two or three key signifiers of power. The backdrop was often minimal, with one or two clues of the international-style city office in which these people operated. The movements of the 4″ × 5″ were adjusted to thin this Polaroid paper-tiger out a little. The subject lent forward into the camera, a sharp unquivering gaze above two large hands ennobled with gold rings and watches. Shot on a wide angle to make their hands appear muscular and workerish, one eyebrow was raised to add the final panache of the cosmopolitan capitalist.

The closer you go to the centre of the power of our age, capital, the more the images portray pure power. I held the darkslides and looked on amazed at the disintegrating state of these 'captains of industry'. People who were, despite their positions, falling apart became, first in the Polaroid and then in the large-format transparency, bastions of symmetry, order and power. This was an important lesson. I realised that the photographer should understand, first and foremost, the political use-value of an image *before* it is shot. The purpose, orbit and distribution of the image were key considerations decided on before the image was shot, not after. The photography in this instant worked for the photographer, for the subject, and for whom it was commissioned because it created a vision of the subject in accord with their professional purpose (making money, controlling stock, asset-stripping, etc.) rather than their actual physical self. In the image, they were auditioning for the part of themselves as myth. What was interesting for me was the process by which this 'positive' image came into existence. It seemed that I had witnessed the bones of a process which might be reworkable in a different context and produce more radical results.

The use of a 4" × 5", Polaroid monitoring and the like in the process of the portrayal of capital, in this instance, were key factors in bringing the subjects (the owners or managers of the means of production, distribution and exchange), into a consciousness whereby they understood their role as a social actor of their power position. Conversely, in much reportage of the left, a 'dialectically' opposite process of non-consultation, victim-positioning 35mm photography has been developed. As the captains of industry were in crisp, full colour 4" × 5",[2] so those oppressed by industry and society were shown in uprated 1600ASA grainy black-and-white 'realism'.[3] It is perverse but true that the first 'right-wing' process held more political potential for the portrayal of disabled people than the second 'left-wing' process. Of course, there are elements of necessity with black-and-white photography, it is a cheaper process and much non-market-based editorial work and papers were printed in black-and-white. Also, the rates of pay are lower[4] the further away from the commercial and fashion magazines, which puts pressure on the photographer to move fast.

Nevertheless, the expediency of the process in left reportage combined with the need for proof of the evilness of 'the system' has created victim-positioning. Most photographers are not recording life which is within their own experience and are essentially voyeuristic. As I have pointed out in Chapters 3, 4 and 5, the reportage pursuit of the damned symbol-as-evidence plunges deepest in its portrayal of disabled people. These were the discourses of photography which I understood when I received a commission from Camerawork Gallery, London, to work as one of four photographers/photography groups exploring issues in the representation of disabled people.

My work in A Sense of Self began with myself. I applied for one of the commissions to look at open and hidden disability. A 'hidden disability' is a label which is wrapped around people whose impairments are not visually received. Non-disabled people expect those of us with these types of impairments not to witness our impairment or disablement. Out of their sight, out of our mind? We are constructed as refugees at the border between disability and non-disability. The guards survey us and issue passports into the promised land if we agree to internalise our oppression or pretend that it doesn't exist. Many people with hidden impairments feel close enough to the promised (non-disabled) land to attempt to 'pass'. In the commission, I wanted to undo the notion that epilepsy was hidden. Also, I wanted to make it clear that epilepsy was an impairment which did not come and go but which was permanent. When the tide is out the ocean does not disappear.

To begin with, the aim of A Sense of Self [5] was to create positive images of disabled people. Positive images are only effective and, indeed, only have meaning if there is a real power-base for them to 'speak' for, and which is challenging the oppressive power-base on a wider level *beyond* representation. Imagery can be a developed manifestation of that struggle. It can also lay down clues, even a map, towards a future. Positive imagery can create a vision which can be forged into the physical. This, to me, is its purpose. In this sense then, I saw (and still see) myself as working to visualise the politics, celebration and empowerment of disabled people by the disability movement.

In each shoot, the large-format camera was set up with studio lights on either side of it. Whether it was with an individual or a group, the same view was maintained so that the subject moved into or out of the view at will. It was important that the camera desisted from its traditional roving position. This decreased the passivity of the subjects who normally might be waiting for something to go snap. In physically occupying one arena at a time, the process came to echo drama rather than reportage.

The large-format slow photographic process suited the project. Colour representation and the representation of power were important issues if we were to work against traditional black-and-white oppressive imagery. Victim positioning of those I worked with would also have meant self-oppression. Although it is not unheard of for like to exploit like, my own self-discovery was completely bound up in the discovery of others like myself. In this sense, the process was shamanistic. It was a process of co-discovery and of a sharing of the wounds.[6]

Clearly, looking at the images (Plates 15, 16, 17 and 18), the direct-to-camera gaze came into play. The holiday snap dialogue between the photographer and subject underpinned the images. The eyes of the subject confront the viewer and challenge the notion of unconscious dependency prevalent in most disability portrayal. It seemed to me that disabled people had been used as the enfleshing of discourses in which they had neither power nor rights to representational control. The object of the direct gaze in this work, then, was to acknowledge the conscious involvement in the process by the sitter/subject. The confidence of occupation of the image by the subject was worked on in several previous sessions, both of photography and taped interviews, in which people laid down their own vision and sense of self. A common thread which emerged was the person's relationship with his or her impairment. The move from medical model to social model was not simply the switching of abstract models. It seemed to me important to use portrait photography to show people's impairment, for example the damage caused during a seizure, *without showing victims*. This perhaps is one of the essential differences with the impairment charities, apart from the more obvious ones like colour versus black-and-white, and so on.

The psychic journey of transforming my and others' self-loathing into self-love (or, at least, self-respect) was played out in the photographic workshop environment which I created with the people whom I photographed in A Sense of Self. In meeting and working with other people with epilepsy, I met myself in different forms and I met others who felt parts of me reflected them. There were difficulties. In pulling down our own Berlin Walls, it was sometimes hard to sense the boundaries or to breathe. Neither I nor the people with whom I worked, bar one, were at that point trained workshop leaders. Notions of boundaries, separateness and private space were thrown out the window in a furious rush to find new forms of representation which spoke to us and others. I was not quite sure of the difference between paraphernalia and tools, but the lack of boundaries, despite the drawbacks, produced a warmth and a nearness of the subject which itself was a vital asset in forming new disability imagery.

Striking Poses (Plates 6–14) was commissioned by the Graeae Theatre Company, Britain's only all-disabled theatre company, to explore the relationship between identity, imagery and theatre.[7] This provided an opportunity to explore further some of the connections between photographic process and the politics of disabled identity. In this commission, I worked with the Graeae Theatre in Education Group in two segregated schools in London. The theatre group worked with the children for a number of weeks using theatre techniques to explore the construction of identity and self. The work I did was one session per week in each school over a period of six weeks.

The 4″ × 5″ camera was set up precisely in the same position each week for the whole of the session. It was made clear that, again, the camera would not be a roving eye waiting for them to laugh or cry. They were not going to be captured. If they did not want to be photographed, that was up to them. The Theatre in Education Group continued to develop workshop techniques and games which dealt with story-telling and so on, and the photography came at the end of each session. The children moved into the visual arena much like entering a stage. They were shown the similarities between photography and drama through the use of Polaroid feedback. Each person was photographed as they wished and then the Polaroid produced was discussed. I used black-and-white Polaroid type 55, which produced a positive and negative. The Polaroid positive was given to the sitter, and the negative was used to blow up the image for the following week's session.

The actual act of exposing the Polaroid positive negative was the last stage in a process of image-making and body language development. I was approaching disability representation from the point of view of the subject and saw my job in this project as that of a director focusing an actor in the role of a real or idealised self. The images explored how the body language of the disabled person could be mobilised to speak against the slug-like portrayal of disabled people in other forms of representation. It was crucial that the children could accept, reject or react to the images acted out by them and shot by me. Furthermore, the use of Polaroid levelled any internal hierarchies the group may have had in terms of the degree of mental disablement, degree of impairment, and so on because of the relative accessibility of visuals as opposed to ideas based in text. It would be foolish to say all are equal in the eye of the camera, but as a non-verbal tool of communication, it certainly levelled other cultural differences.

After three sessions in each school, the Theatre in Education Group and I conducted a workshop exploring both charity advertising and the black-and-white portraits we had done so far. Charity advertising was rejected by the children, and so was, with less ferocity, the black-and-white work we had done! Black-and-white did not reflect their common photographic currency, which was the colour snapshot. We then moved into colour. The narrative of visual literacy was anchored into the series by the presence in the colour images of their black-and-white predecessors. The confidence of the children with the camera and their own image had grown out of the black-and-white Polaroiding and the first colour images show this shedding of a representational skin.

I wanted to anchor into the images signifiers which told the viewer that these images were drama as much as naturalism, and that the key to creating empowering imagery was in the process by which it was made as much as its moral or political intentions. The blue backdrop was brought in as both a stage and to create the Brechtian *Verfremdung*, an alienation device. The staging occurred at the borders between the backdrop and the classroom to show a relationship or clash between naturalism and drama. Again, at the prompting of the children, the camera was pulled back and they entered the arena in groups rather than singly, culminating in the final anarchic and celebratory image. I think the work is successful because it shows both a form of image-making *and* the image-contents themselves and thus demonstrates a method of creating positive images of disabled people who are conscious, no matter what their disablement, of their involvement.

The rejection by disabled people, the disability movement and its allies of the irredeemably redundant forms of charity advertising and the like has created a visual vacuum strangely devoid of photographic and representational boundaries or rules. While it was clear that certain practices were not wanted, this does not in itself deliver acceptable forms. Many non-disabled photographic observers continued to practise, to use Jo Spence's term, as social workers with cameras. They found that their positions of objective distance or patronising intervention produced images they recognised, but which spoke to nobody else (least of all, the disability movement). Like flies bewildered by panes of glass, non-disabled photographers cannot move forward beyond the old forms. It seems to me, in A Sense of Self and Striking Poses that the difference between this work and other more oppressive disability photography was the difference between observation and engagement. To move from an observer to an engager, for me, lay in the process of image-making and in the identification of the photographer.

This issue of form and content, of representation and process, is as old as the mind/body split of patriarchal culture itself, which is perhaps where the seeing/feeling divide began.[8] From the Socratic questioning process towards truth-finding, through the Renaissance to Brechtian drama, to the theoretical work of Victor Burgin, the issue of the knowledgeable or communicative value of forms, areas and processes of representation has been discussed and explored. Within my fine art training, these issues had been mused upon and argued over *ad infinitum*. The purpose of these debates has often been to find forms of pure beauty or pure abstract meaning. The very isolation and social irrelevancy of the ideas was paradoxically a sign of their purpose and success. Although I finally ground to a halt with these abstract aesthetical debates (so long as they remained untied to the politics of need), I understood that narrative and process in the making of representation were problematical and that both had to be critically engaged in the production of radical photography if the new representations had any chance of communicating wider issues at all.

It seemed to me, then, that a key possibility within the breaking down of the old medical order of disability (and how to represent disabled people beyond this form), was in the historical shifting of accepted forms away from their previous contexts and certainties. If colour denoted power, and we wanted power, then we must use this form. If black-and-white had been oppressive, and we wanted to show the movement away from oppression, have colour rise from black-and-white. If disabled people appear confused by the camera, and therefore are read as socially confused by the viewer, use Polaroid feedback to break this negative gaze. If disabled people's consciousness of their image ranges between charity advertising and the family album, with almost nothing in between, then reconstruct these two forms into a third positive form. If shooting down to the eyes of disabled people denoted disempowerment, then shoot up to the eyes. The positive-image effectiveness would be in the reclamation, entry and positioning of the work in the wider disability discourse in new ways which, by their very presence, suggest that new forces are happening. (Incidentally, the reason my work has not concentrated on 'the picket line' image of fighting disability is precisely because I believe that new forms of representation do not have to nail the narrative to the obvious. Their very presence in the institutions of power would suggest that a wider social change is happening.)

So I came to Beyond the Barriers: Disability, Sexuality and Personal Relationships (Plates 19–24).[9] Each project, each commission, allowed me to develop a general social model of disability imagery, which is to say a shift away from the biological certainty of oppression within the medical model of disability and its attendant structured dependency, infantilism and so on, through exploring a range of forms and forces which might be either new or old, but which could be given new meanings in new contexts. However, none of this 'post-modernist' shifting of meaning and form could have happened without the presence of the disability movement. Within the workshop space which I continued to create, for the most part, with the people with whom I worked, the private exploration which led to the social orbit of the images was conducted on a personal and subjective basis. It was about feelings, moods, fantasies, as much as politics, gossip and the ins and outs of disability culture.

I did not enter the arena with a visual preconception and position people as valiant comrades or the heroic fallen. I felt able to admit into that photographic space a cornucopia which contained subjective identity, inner vision, story-telling of pain, objective ideology and the physical here and now. I don't mean that I was a scholar in each of those areas, I just mean that in my life I had inhabited references, theories and identities from many areas which I then brought to the image-making arena. I have never been in co-counselling but I imagine the process of mutual recognition and trust which allowed out voices and ghosts from within the sitter/subject and from within myself might be similar.

In Beyond the Barriers, for which mine was one of three commissions, I continued exploring the relationship of colour to narrative, of disabled people's relationship to themselves, to society and to their impairment. I also looked at ways of further developing constructed or dramatic naturalism: my 'decisive moment' here was the clash between naturalism and staging. I wanted to do a series of images that worked individually but that also linked up. The relationship of the individual to the mass or to the movement as an issue has a long history in socialism and I wanted to look at this issue. Also, I began to develop a theme which had lain more quietly in my previous work, that of the difficult relationship between oppression and positive imagery. It has been a legitimate criticism of positive imagery that it can hide the oppression in its glorification of the overcoming of disabling barriers. It can lay out the possibilities of a future while ignoring, perhaps even suppressing, the here and now.

I conducted taped interviews with the sitters, as I had in other work, and played back the tape over and over again until I identified a key element. I did not shoot many Polaroids (when I did, it was with people who did not know me politically or who had expressed a wish to work that way) but showed people a portfolio outlining forms and methods and the politics of disability representation. Either quotes from the taped interviews or passages written by the sitters themselves accompanied the images. The relationship was a critical one. More than in previous work, I wanted the text to take some of the narrative responsibility of the image and allow the image to move further into photo-drama and magic superrealism.

I produced a series of eight images which began with low washed-out browns and moved through a fragmented and brittle alchemy to a crescendo of high, full colours. The use of colour in each case underwrote the story in the image and text. The beginning work was shot close to the subject and I wanted to show the individuals' stories, at this end of the work, in a quite tight, even minimalist, way. The camera then pulls gradually away throughout the series of eight to show, in high-colour glory, visions of the subjects and their stories. Some of the images show an unproble-matic superworld of bliss and harmony – these come in the high colour range – while others engage in naming the oppression of the subject without victim-positioning them. In a sense, I was making forays back into oppressive imagery in order to rework it politically. Two images which demonstrate this are *Anonymous: Epilepsy and Sexual Abuse* (Plate 20) and *Chris Davies, TV Presenter* (Plate 22).

In the 'anonymous' image, I worked with a friend who told the story of this condition. The central issue for him was to make public certain aspects of his disablement – in particular, the sexual abuse of people with epilepsy – but to bring this out while keeping the subject both present and hidden. I looked and listened at once. As the sitter told me particular stories of struggle, I watched his body tell the same story in body language. We then explored the relationship between this move-ment and the sitter's feelings and put down some Polaroid exploration markers (Plate 19). In these we looked at ways of technically constructing an image which could relate the story to the sitter and to me. The sitter's story was of a decline, an abyss, a survival and a re-emergence. The monastic simplicity of the sitter's post-prison life was reflected in both attire and language. In his simple story-telling was a complete power. The tonal range, the signs of the body, the signs of the home, the blur of the face, and the sunlight on the sitter through the window emulated the power in the simplicity.

In the second image (Plate 22), that of Chris Davies, we had met a couple of times before the shoot to talk about his story. Again, this was taped and provided the basis for his text. Chris made a point on the tape: he talked about being both stared at and ignored. He developed this to talk about the hegemony of non-disabled body language within sexuality and sexual connections, and his relationship to this as someone with cerebral palsy. The image attempted to develop these issues visually. First, we constructed a stage in a prominent place (London Bridge) behind which walked commuters on their way to the City of London to work. We reversed the perception of movement between non-disabled people and people with cerebral palsy. The passers-by look back but hurry on. The image was shot on a half-second with two flashguns and daylight to capture their 'double-take'. In the issue of being stared at or ignored, Chris had also talked about how his social profile as a TV presenter (BBC's *One-In-Four*) added a different dimension to the staring/ignoring dynamic. I wanted to bring in a *Verfremdung* with the backdrop and mixed lighting to create a studio/street ambiguity with which to look at this issue in the image. The colouring contains a wider range than that of the *Anonymous: Epilepsy and Sexual Abuse* image and this was following a thread through to the psychedelic colours of the last two images which I felt denoted celebration, coming out and power. The growth in colour followed the narrative, as the images show a move out from buildings into social settings, with the final image being of Andrew Miah on the South Africa House Picket.

Plates 25–9 and 46–9 show predominantly black-and-white work commissioned from within the wider voluntary sector, ranging from local authorities to the trade unions. Black-and-white comes back into play and many of the politics of colour representation which I had worked on in the larger commissions are inadmissible under black-and-white. However, it is important to demonstrate that this does not necessarily mean a retreat to oppressive imagery. I could still use a process of image-making which worked more slowly than 35mm reportage and so, for the majority of these commissions, I shot the work on a medium-format Hasselblad and mostly with a standard (80mm) lens. I was careful to avoid 'grainy realism' and used plus-x mostly at normal (125ASA). The films were developed in Agfa Rodinal, sometimes with extended developing times and greater dilutions to soften the tonal differences, and printed on Agfa Record Rapid grade 2.

This formula is more or less constant and, as a jobbing issue-based photographer, I wanted to maintain a consistent technical procedure with a consistent political line. This was not always easy. Many clients saw 'positive images' but wanted to have 'their handicapped' portrayed 'positively', enjoying semi-trained arts workers doing things to them. By and large, I stuck to the notions of positive imagery which I had worked on in the larger commissions: direct gaze to camera showing consciousness of the image-process, which metaphorically translated as consciousness in the wider social arena. I also positioned the camera up to the eyes to break up any victim positioning which might occur at the use-end of the image.

Many commissioning organisations pressured me to show disabled people as passive and happy recipients of their services. While I understand the pressure to be shown to be delivering services to client groups, my position was to show affirmative, positive self-identity within the disabled person. I felt, and still feel, that this message on posters, trade papers and leaflets for which these images were shot, would attract disabled people far more than any which showed gratitude or dependency, no matter how well intentioned by the service provider. However, I am also showing this material in a publication of my work because, quite simply, I feel it is important to show ideological or issue-based work which takes on new forms of representation, however modified for different orbits, within reportage jobbing photography. All photographic discourses are sites of struggle, from the church newsletter to the gallery, and we have to fight in as many as we have access to (and, of course, in those where we don't).[10]

The final work is entitled *The Creatures Time Forgot*. The work and exhibition divides into three parts. The first third is entitled The Process of Disablement. This consists of two major pieces. The first is entitled *The Sites of Disablement* (Plates 34–6). This triptych was a part of a commission for the direct action group, the Construction Safety Campaign, in association with the Connolly Association, who are fighting to decrease the 150 deaths and the hundreds of disablements which occur annually on UK building sites. The organisation is made up almost entirely of construction workers. My brief was to explore different ways of highlighting the issue of construction safety. It was made clear that the CSC were not looking for images which victim-position those working in the appalling conditions, but neither were the conditions to be hidden. The work was commissioned to be shown in exhibition form, with separate images distributed to illustrate articles and as press prints.[11] The text used quotes by the people photographed, which allowed the image-narrative to speak in symbolic and dramatic language as well as in naturalistic language. Again, it was the dialectic between naturalistic and constructed imagery which was used to make the images speak of empowerment and the conscious fightback against the working conditions. The acknowledgement by the subject of the photographic process is the metaphor for their consciousness within the wider political issue.

The second series of The Process of Disablement is entitled The Shifting Sands of HIV (Plates 30–3). This was commissioned by the Institute of Education who asked me to explore new forms of representing HIV and the social disablement. Working closely with one person, Gerry McGraph, we developed a four-part tableau of social shifts and social interaction/social drama of living with HIV. I used the large-format Polaroid type 55, as I had in Striking Poses, and looked at different ways of linking together a narrative of images, while leaving at least one image available in the sequence as a press print or illustrative image.[12] It was important to me that the form of representation that I was working on could be networked in as many photographic arenas as possible. The work begins in black-and-white, moves into deliberately misprocessed, type-55 mask work, then into photo-drama, out into idealism and the super race. Again, as with much of my work, I am looking at processes which name the pain or the oppression but do not construct a victim. The naming of the struggle itself is incompatible, I would argue, with the construction of a victim if the photographer is aligned to the struggle on a personal level. Clearly, one only has to survey the general press to know that many editors and photographers would not hold with this.

The second third of The Creatures is the six-part poster series funded by the Joseph Rowntree Foundation and entitled Liberty, Equality, Disability: Images of a Movement (Plates 37–42). These posters continue the high-energy portraiture of disabled people but, again, posit references to the oppression without constructing victims. The text by the sitter continues to release the image from the constraints of hyper-realism and allow the range of references to expand to the magic-realism which I began to look at in Beyond the Barriers.

The third stage of The Creatures is entitled In the Charity Camp (Plates 43–5). This work, more than any other I have done, re-enters the oppressive imagery of charity advertising but from the position of the likely future of that form. Charity advertising will eventually move into colour as an answer to the criticisms of its black-and-white negativity, but will undoubtedly maintain every other sign and signifier of negativity, dependency and impairment as disability. The models in this work are some of the key activists in the UK disability movement and we made this work in order to explore how to take the fight back into the charity camp. These images, then, are the Trojan Donkey offering from myself and the activists who modelled to the impairment charities. The same methods of high production values, of colour, of photo-drama, have been used but to slightly different ends. I was particularly keen to acknowledge the 'crip' humour so prevalent in the disability arts movement. Beyond basket-weaving and 'being good, being positive' is a dark side of humour born in anger and anarchy. The disability movement, at least in the UK, has not developed an ideological and moral 'line' of pure positivity and self-censure of its members. There are behavioural pressures on disabled people, particularly from the 'new men' and 'new women' allies who appear to support us, to construct such a 'line' in which satire, anger and bile have no place. However, this humour[13] displays the point of contact between the oppression and the point of resistance and is a crucial part of any 'reclaimed' culture. I don't think a body of work in any radical portraiture could be complete without this.

I have been on a journey of representation in which the cross-identity between myself and the people whom I have photographed has been the paramount connection. In discovering that the great unreconstructable abyss of my impairment could be transferred away from my body into the social arena, I picked up my attempts at obliterating the pain and silence I had carried, and brought that process of transformation into the photographic process to exchange with the sitters and subjects with whom I have been privileged to work. I have realised that the fragments and *alter egos* which I attempted to use to mask the central crisis of my impairment only came to real life once that crisis had been named, converted and empowered. Where once they danced around in escapist chaos, they came to dance around in the photographic workshop process as choices and relationships. If I feel I have brought anything to disability photography in particular, and photography in general, it is that I have worked photography to expand people, not restrict them.

7

Revolt of the species!

A THEORY OF THE SUBJECT

A burgeoning of photographic theory occurred in the early to mid-1980s, with literature ranging from Susan Sontag's *On Photography*,[1] Roland Barthes's *Camera Lucida*,[2] through the work in the UK by Victor Burgin and the Image/Text school, with books like *Thinking Photography*[3] and *The End of Art Theory*,[4] then on to the work by Photography Workshop and the Photography/Politics[5] series, to the work of Jo Spence and *Putting Myself in the Picture*,[6] which was published in 1986. On the other side of the Atlantic, people like Allan Sekula, whose *Photography Against the Grain*[7] was published in 1984, developed similar 'deconstructivist' critiques of the photographic image and representation.

These publications ranged from works on high scholastic theory and practice to those on interventionist auto-portraiture theory and practice. As a 'movement' it broadly represented the breakdown in the modernist belief within photographic practice of the epistemological and self-referential sovereignty of the single photographic image. The ability of the photographic image to impart 'its' information or meaning by means of fixed and universal signs and symbols was proved, at least theoretically, to be a fallacy. In the UK, Burgin in particular marked the high theoretical point of this deconstruction of modernist notions of image-information with two publications: *Thinking Photography* (1982), which he edited, and *The End of Art Theory*, which was a collection of essays he wrote between 1976 and 1985.

Burgin, in particular, located meaning *not* within the surface of an image but within the context and the discourse in which the image is positioned. Drawing on the general discourse of *meaning* within culture, history and society, with sources ranging from Saussure to Barthes, from Marx to feminism, from Freud to Lacan, he laid down one of the key tenets of post-modernist theory: namely, that the sign, the signifier and the signified have no automatic or inherent universal meaning. The signifier is the object, the signified is what it symbolises and the sign is the 'thing' which synthesises the two. As Judith Williamson put it, 'These [terms] are only divided for analytical purposes; in practice a sign is always a thing-plus-meaning.'[8] For the purposes of this book, this analysis is important because it led Burgin to assert that there was no such thing as a positive or a negative image as such.

> To be quite explicit: such 'racism' or 'sexism' as we may ascribe to these or other images is not 'in' the photographs themselves. Such 'isms', in the sphere of representation, are a complex of texts, rhetorics, codes, woven into the fabric of the popular preconscious.[9]

Meaning may be anchored, in the way that an advertising image is anchored by a caption, but even then the meaning of the image exists because of the 'closure' by the text of the reading of other meanings by the consumer of the image. The text therefore appears to act as the policer of the meaning in the image. The textual anchor, the policer, itself does not have an unproblematical relationship with the image and therefore its role of anchoring meaning cannot be formally assumed. What prevents the image from descending into a cacophony of meaninglessness is the presence of positions of consciousness of the signs, signifiers and the signified *within the reader (that is, the viewer)*. This consciousness, this ability to read coherence into free form, is based, according to Burgin, in any number of discourses (or social texts) which oscillate within the consciousness of the consumer/reader. *Desire in consumption* rather than *intention in production* becomes, for Burgin, the site of any synthesis or meaning 'in' the image. The projection of meaning into the image by the viewer/reader joins with its surrounding social and representational discourse. The image is 'invaded' by meanings which cross its plastic borders and bring meaning on to the plastic surface itself. The entry of meanings may range from social discourses, 'common sense', as in the 'old bag' image of Gary Winogrand, to the projection of desire into the sign, like the transfer of the Oedipal crisis in men on to images of women in pornography, for example.

The image then is a 'complex of texts'. Taking on much of the conceptualist work of the 1970s, Burgin explores the nature of the text of the image, that is, its 'scripto-visual' meaning, within the space between the image and those who consume or 'read' it, not within the plastic occurrence of the image itself. So, space and the image surround become the site, the entry into the image. The work of Burgin and others asks us to make a quantum leap from reading imagery meaning in two dimensions to reading imagery meaning in multiples of at least three dimensions, expanding *ad infinitum*. We are asked to move off the image to the surround. Does this mean, therefore, that the photographic content of a charity advert is only 'oppressive' because of the written textual 'closure' of meaning in the image? Is it that the photographic image is 'negative' because of the general lack of socialscape surrounding the disabled person, into which floats unnamed (but projected into by non-disabled readers their own disavowal and anxiety) spirits?

This may be true but it is limited. In the final analysis, Burgin absents the relevance of the actual plastic photographic image altogether. If its meaning is *solely* located in the discourses which surround it, then the image itself cannot interrupt or challenge its discursive environment. The black hole in the deconstructive photographic universe of Burgin is that he fails to name *precisely* what *effect* the physical existence of the plastic image has on its discursive (social, political, ideological, psychological or whatever) environment. If it is a mirror of webs which surround it, then what role does the mirror play? In breaking up the 'grand narratives' of self-referential, self-meaningfulness of photography, Burgin himself creates a grand narrative, a singular universe of purposelessness for the image itself.

This is his achievement, but it is also his limitation. The notion of meaning in context is vital but perhaps not so revolutionary. It asks producers and consumers to examine image meaning *in the process* rather than in the single image. This is important but is hardly different from other process theorists and artists, like, for example, Brecht and process theatre. The difference, of course, is that Brecht *accepted* the presence of a relatively fixed historical meaning in the general currency and circulation of signs, especially popular culture, in his theatre whereas Burgin would not do the same in his photography. Indeed, in the space between publishing *Thinking Photography* (1982) and *The End of Art Theory* (1986), Burgin clearly moves away from the needs of *mobilised* photographic theory, that which works in the service of a political movement or cause, to *pure* photographic theory, or that which in itself has no political or ideological anchor as such.

The issue for political photography and, in the case of this book disability photography, is to rework aspects of photographic theory within *mobilised* political action. Reading the literature quoted at the beginning of this chapter, you will witness an increase in the contexting of a wider social politics in photographic practice, as you witness an attendant increase in the positioning of the self of the author in the text. Burgin, in particular, leaves his self out of the text of *The End of Art Theory* (although he concedes in passing that he must be in there somewhere on some level) until the very end when he says

> The end of the 'grand narratives' does not mean the end of either morality or *memory*. For example, to speak personally, the fact that I do not see in contemporary events the portents of the imminent collapse of capitalism and the guarantee of the inevitable triumph of the proletariat does not mean that I have forgotten the experiences of my working-class childhood, it does not erase my sense of what social injustice is, and it does not change my social and political allegiances.[10]

As poignant as this is, it presents a problem for Burgin for a number of reasons. His whole book comes close to stating that mobilised political imagery (propaganda, for example) is impossible on any level. He argues that there is no such thing as reality without representation, that representational forms *themselves* do not have fixed meanings, therefore it must be finally impossible to use imagery to represent the reality of a physical political struggle, be it class, race, disablement and so on. For him to slip in at the end an unproblematised autobiographical badge of identity distinctly trips up his 'objective' construction of a humanly-uninhabited representational universe. He has not linked representation with 'my sense of what social injustice is'.

His 'social and political allegiances' are not named and he does not address his personal and representational entry into them. Burgin does call upon feminist theory in *The End of Art Theory* but he does not actually make the link between the personal and the political.

Here is the rub. The use-value of much photo-theory for the development of a radical disability photographic practice lies in the degree of the inhabitation of the photographic theory by the author/photographer. The placing of the body and the self in the text concurs, in the publications named at the beginning of this chapter, with the extent of the allegiance of the author with expressed political agendas. This is regardless of modernist or post-modernist positions. It begins to show in the work of Allan Sekula, who states quite categorically that he feels his theories cannot proceed without the naming of his self.[11] He tells us that he felt the only way

> to 'account' for my politics – the only way to invite a political dialogue – was to 'begin' with my own class and family background. *Aerospace Folktales* was structured around a movement between mock-sociological distance and familiarity. Certainly it is impossible to escape or ignore the fact that this work is about the conditions of my own upbringing and those of my siblings. And to some extent the class anger discovered in the work – the sense of one's parents' lives being caught within what Ernest Mandel has termed the 'permanent arms economy' of late capitalism – mixes with filial anger and desire.

Sekula covers similar terrain to Burgin but from the position of a Marxist working within post-modernist photographic practice. Sekula explores how images within discourses (which he defines as 'an area of information exchange') are defined not as a void but as an 'incomplete utterance, a message that depends on some external matrix of conditions and presuppositions for its readability'. However, Sekula 'refuses to separate the image from the notion of *task*' (my italics) and quite correctly states that *discourses set the task of the image*. This can be seen in how advertising is used to sell cars, or images of moon-landings tell citizens of the triumph of 'their' countries' systems, and so on. Here we are moving into a notion of intervention in the creation and distribution of image meaning. Allan Sekula's work is premised on the necessity of consciousness of context, not on the praise of the single image.

Without doubt, Jo Spence and *Putting Myself in the Picture* has taken further the intertwining of photographic theory and practice, through the fusion of the personal and the political within the optics of production. Her work charts the movement from that of observer who stands at the edge of the abyss but dare not enter to that of one who goes through what she now terms 'radical ventriloquism' into a photo-drama of the self. Her work, particularly the phototherapy imagery, deals directly with a visual/textual dialogue with the self, whose audience internalises the meaning through their own survivorship (or not) of the same crisis. The drama of phototherapy is a drama of experience. She becomes both past and present, present and past, in a catalogue of political reclamation. The images are often in sequences which help to control the reading of her 'selves' as the daughter, the mother, the father, the worker, the cancer-system survivor, and so on. Burgin's notion of meaning within the discourse was for him an endpoint. For Jo Spence, it is a point of departure.

For me and my practice and, I would argue, general political imagery including disability imagery, photographic practice which explores visually and textually (accepting their relative interchangeability) a theory of production and consumption, which names the *intention* and *task* of the image and which, finally, politically locates the person in the image and text is a prerequisite of outsider photography. The final anchor in this *photopolitik* is memory. It is the rising degrees of the admission of individual/collective memory into photographic theory and practice by which we might recognise its mobilised purpose. The free-floating meaning 'in' an image becomes anchored by the identification by the consumer (the reader) and the producer (the writer) of signs which mark similar journeys, experiences and memory.

It is the artist's/photographer's/propagandist's job to name these journeys, experiences and memories in terms of a '*scrip*to-visual' language of signs and signifiers within the images, so that the consumer/reader can experience himself/herself in viewing the image. If we are to create political disability imagery which mobilises disabled people into self-love and action, then the dual process of subjective and objective identification is vital. This is a long way from the standard left 'dialectical' imagery of 'struggle' v. 'victim' observed abstractedly (the Miranda syndrome) which essentially fails because the viewer can pity but not become. The position of total victim is unlivable in. As James Baldwin put it, 'The victim who is able to articulate the situation of the victim has ceased to be a victim; he, or she, has become a threat.'[12]

So, how does this work in the disability *realpolitik*? Arguably, one of the key battles for the disability movement on the issue of disability representation came when the King's Fund Centre organised a conference on disability imagery entitled 'Putting People in the Brief' in 1989. This was to be the back-up and confirmation of the consultancy paper entitled 'They Are Not in the Brief' written by non-disabled disability consultant Susan Scott-Parker. Both 'dealt with' disability representation but, as both titles suggest, the nearest this came to be named was in a 'they'. The issue of disability imagery in charity advertising was to be discussed and several prominent members of both the charitable and advertising sectors were invited. Certain disabled people were invited while others, who had clearly been involved in the politics of disability representation but who might widen the remit beyond the 'reformist' agenda of the day, were not.

This, however, changed. Some of us who were not initially invited to the seminar called a meeting to which disabled people who had been invited and disabled people who had not been invited to the King's Fund Conference came. Non-disabled allies like Camerawork attended.[13] It was important to build on the links between the disability movement and allies and prevent the charities, to use Aneurin Bevan's joke, from claiming medals from the battles they lost! I wrote a series of demands which the group endorsed. These we intended to distribute at the conference if we did gain admittance, or to distribute from a picket line if we didn't.

We demanded that any charity advertising guidelines should be written and controlled by disabled people and we pointed out that charities and ad agencies would never change their advertising without the employment of disabled people in positions of power at all levels of the process. We insisted that a fundamental shift of power to disabled people and away from charity had to be based on the social model of disability and 'be adopted throughout the concepts and thinking of charities'.[14] The demands continued to state that the disability issue was one of rights, not of charity, and that the charities and their advertising were not incidental nor were they working for us. They were a key site of struggle when they 'project through their very influential poster-campaigns negative stereotypes of isolated hopelessness'. The eight-point paper continued to take apart the smug self-congratualising feel of the day, and ended with the demand that the King's Fund Centre support disabled controlled solutions to charity advertising and not sponsor yet more non-disabled control dressed up as help. As I put it at the time, 'Remember, Othello was black, not blacked-up!'

An ad hoc committee was formed by disabled people and planned to picket the seminar to force changes. However, those of us who were initially considered non-desirable were suddenly invited. Although still a significant minority, the day was an important struggle and a success from our point of view. It undoubtedly created a lot of animosity but resulted in the King's Fund Centre agreeing to fund the Disabled-Only Ad Hoc Group (renamed as the Media Images Group and affiliated to the British Council of Organisations of Disabled People) to set up a steering group and commission a research document outlining a code of ethics for the portrayal of disabled people in charity advertising and the media. This report by Colin Barnes[15] pulls together ideas of what makes a disability image negative or positive within the media, then it outlines the structure by which disabled and non-disabled people can read the signs. This structure will provide markers for complaints, for example. There is no doubt that this document will provide an important text for controlling future charity advertising.

It appears that the mountain has indeed come to Mohammed. However, although image guidelines and ethics are an important area of disability intervention, it has to be remembered that as a critical response to an oppressive form, they are unlikely to contain a process for the counter-formation of alternative imagery. Their site of struggle is still within 'the belly of the beast', critiquing images set within oppressive structures. That notwithstanding, and given that 'ethics' are unlikely to contain the depth of critical analysis that other photographic theory and practice contain, they are none the less a political step forward because they are mobilised by the 'task' of the disability movement, whereas the previous photographic theory described, no matter how important it might be, is generally not. Codes, ethics, critiques and so on which seek to change non-disabled controlled disability/impairment imagery are welcomed because they establish the issue of representation in many parties' minds, but their ability to shift the balance of power towards disabled people and disabled people's cultural representation is unlikely to be within the ethics themselves.

And of course, the setting-up of non-statutory codes, ethics and voluntary self-regulation by charities and others may be particularly welcomed, but probably further softened, by non-disabled people. Most charities and voluntary sector organisations recognise that there is no way forward other than reform, but they do so under silent protest. The 'bargain',[16] if we are not extremely careful, will be struck. The bargain, as Paul Logmore has pointed out,[17] is that the access struggle is not named, physical barriers are not named, and the disability 'problem' is discussed in the realm of 'attitudes'. The positive representation bargain, with the charities' endorsement of the code of ethics, is that they will 'positively' represent impairments if we agree not to represent charities as disablers! The representational bargain met its historical height with the acceptance by the American people of disabled president Franklin Delano Roosevelt. Of the 35,000 photographs of President Roosevelt, only two (and these were never published) showed him seated in his wheelchair.[18] Roosevelt and the media correctly understood the power of photography in the representation, or not in this case, of disablement and constructed a structured absence of his impairment or disablement worthy of Stalin's exit of Trotsky from images of the Bolshevik Revolution. There can be no doubt that Roosevelt, from the time he contracted polio in 1921 to his death in 1945, not only acquiesced in this vision of himself but acquiesced 'positively'. The reformation of oppressive imagery is only important (or, at least, more than superficially) if it is linked to wider social issues, such as access.

Codes of ethics have to be clear whether they are asking non-disabled organisations to be 'positive' about the impairment or 'positive' about the disablement and what a positive (or, for that matter, negative) relationship to each really is. 'Positive' should mean the naming of the site of struggle and the group's or individual's relationship to it. 'Positive' should not be the denial, disavowal or suppression of the struggle and oppression. Of course, the reality of positive imagery is that it is not a free-floating self-referential form. Its meaning is anchored in its context, distribution and *task*. Therefore, the issue of disability representation has to be tied to the general movement for rights. If non-disabled organisations do support our representational struggles, and there are clear signs that this is happening,[19] then we have to build into this support a 'clause' whereby image-politics become a part of the struggle for access, not an excuse for it. Otherwise, the replacement of the issue of 'attitudes' for the issue of access will be echoed by the replacement of plastic images for physical access.

Clearly, we are in an inherently passive and unstable position if we remain *exclusively* in the approval/disapproval relationship to charity and media disability imagery. In a sense, this position is the classic position of most viewers and consumers of photographic imagery, even those who take their own images. Barthes wrote that photography and the photograph, like original (that is, historical) theatre, record the relationship of the dead to the living. In photography, all that is photographed is dead in the sense that it has passed on.[20] The visual moment reflected back to us is a reflection of something past. It is from this position of reading, which must affect all those who consume imagery, that the roots of the passivication of disabled people in relation to oppressive disability imagery are entwined with the existing physical marginalisation which the charities and other forms of non-disabled representation practise. There is nothing fatalistic in this position, the important thing is to be aware of it and to question what is to be done about it.

The role of disabled groups such as the BCODP Media Images group is clearly to challenge the 'tragedy principle' of the media and charity portrayal of disabled people. However, the pressure-group position is not enough. Disabled people have given notice of a refusal to occupy the victim position. We, as disabled people, have become a threat. This threat has to be converted into power and analysis. Not for nothing is the lesbian symbol a double-headed axe. We need a two-pronged approach. One head of our axe is the 'ethics' pressure cited previously. The other might be the further intervention in the image discourse from the position of the subject. The root of this process lies more in radical drama theory than photographic theory.

Barthes was right to view the origins of photography as a derivation not of painting, which it is generally thought to have usurped,[21] but of theatre.[22] Crucially, while Barthes explores meaning and memory and death, read on the surface of the images (particularly one of his mother, who had died just before he wrote *Camera Lucida*), he does not investigate the process of theatre within photography from the point of view of subject, namely those observed. He does not explore a way into imagery from beneath the surface and in front of the optics. Photographic critics have constantly discussed images above the surface and behind the optics exclusively on the level of surface or of its wider discursive environment. For example, Burgin took *Camera Lucida* to task because, he says, it anchors meaning through 'an evocation of *intentionality* as it strives to conjure the image of a loved person through the intermediary ("medium") of a snapshot'.[23] Although Burgin concedes that the book is significant for photographic theory precisely because of the 'active participation of the viewer in producing the meaning/effect of the photograph' he pulls *Camera Lucida* back from something which is engaged in the living meaning of the subject in images to an artefact which is observed abstractly. This process of creating two-dimensionality representation from three-dimensionality reality is continually discussed in photographic theory at the level of representation, that is, at the level of two dimensions. This has led to the development of an essentially *unmobilised* (i.e. outside the political forces of the day) position for much photographic theory and practice. While much of this theory is disengaged (although, of course, this does not invalidate it) it blocks off an essential route to radical disability photography because it has no notion of *performance*. So, how people enter, control or direct imagery as subjects is the key route which has remained unnamed, even silenced, within much radical photography.[24] To develop this we have to look outside most photographic discourse theory and explore a representational medium which has had, over the last twenty years, a far more radical history regarding the role of *subject* than that of photography. That form is radical drama and within it an examination of the three tenets crucial to a truly radical disability photography can be found. The three tenets are: (1) a theory of the subject (i.e. those surveyed and their control and positioning); (2) a theory of the tragedy principle (and routes beyond it); and (3) a theory of the process of representational production.

The playwright Ionesco said of his plays that he was inventing a new language that everyone speaks already.[25] In this simple statement lies a summing-up of the mission and purpose of much radical theatre. From Brecht to Gay Sweatshop, alternative theatre has attempted to create plays which, in specifically speaking the language of their audience, spoke back to the audience a political narrative of the consumers' subjectivity and experiences which they may or may not have grasped previously or seen represented. Unlike photographic representation, theatrical representation is consumed more or less at the point of production by its audience. The major difference between the two forms of radical theatre and radical photography is the vicinity of the audience.

Whereas consumption of the product has been as vague to independent photography as the ghost of his father was to Hamlet, becoming the stuff more of existential *Angst* than practical consideration, the politics of the consumption of drama is inherent within the presence of the audience. While this is not an unproblematical relationship, it does set up the conditions for a dialogic or dialectical (or both) approach to representation, and no post-Brechtian radical drama has proceeded without taking on board this issue.

Augusto Boal, in particular, has analysed how theatre may either pacify or mobilise its audience. In his view, tragedy is the key element of the depoliticisation (that is, the denial that politics is inherent in all forms, including drama) of most drama. Taking an overview of radical drama, one can see that the single most important characteristic in radical theatre is this rejection of *tragedy in favour of mobilisation*. It goes without saying that this rejection is also an important characteristic of the disability movement with its rejection of the 'tragic' medical view of disability, the 'tragic' portrayal of disabled people in charity advertising, and so on. Radical theatre practice and theory is one of the most important areas of representation for disabled people and disability photography precisely because of the specificity of *tragedy* as a key site, perhaps *the* key site, of struggle.[26]

It is this form of tragedy (which imbues practically all non-radical theatre representation *and* much photographic representation, particularly of disabled people) which Augusto Boal has explored.[27] He firmly anchors the development of this form within the material relations of the Ancient Greek world (where 90 per cent of the people were slaves) and says that 'The tragic hero appears when the state begins to utilize the theater for the political purpose of coercion of the people.' But how is this 'coercion' effected?

Boal maps a move-by-move breakdown of the aesthetics of tragedy. First, enter the tragic hero. He is not initially revealed as tragic. The character acts two aspects: one is the ethos in the action, while the other is the thought which determines the action. Together, the aspects constitute the development of the action by the character. They appear inseparable but in the ethos appears 'the whole of the faculties, passions and habits'.[28] All of these must appear good, *except one*. This must be bad. It is on to the bad part, the bad ethic, that the moral, political and ethical codes of the social order of the day will be projected. This part is outside the law. To hide the political discourse represented by this site, this impurity, it will be made a tragic flaw. This will become the site of the struggle. Either it must be destroyed or it will destroy society. What Boal calls the *Hamartia*, comes to cause conflict. As he puts it, 'it is the only trait that is not in harmony with what society regards as desirable.'[29] Since the audience does not want to be undesirable, they 'assume a passive attitude and delegate the power of action to the character'.[30] Without acting, they live, fear, love and hate through the character as delegate. Empathy comes through the identification of their fears with those of the character, their hates with the character's hates, and so on. The empathy takes place both in terms of what the character does, their ethos, and why they do it, their reason, because both the character and the audience occupy the same social codes, ethics, laws and so on.

The character begins in hope. He or she 'follow[s] an ascending path toward happiness, accompanied empathetically by the spectator'. Then the character recognises an error, a flaw, through which the spectator recognises her or his own flaws and errors. Then comes the catastrophe, the price of the error and flaw. This is often the character's death or the death of his loved ones. The spectator, terrified by the price of the error, is purified of this fear by having seen it lived out dramatically. This is tragic theatre. It is here that, according to Boal, the audience is coerced into antipolitics. Theatre was the dominant form of representation in Ancient Greece and the tragic theatre (which of course represented social existence) was construed as having nothing to do with politics. Reality is represented as tragedy, which is the theatre of doom for those who transgress.

The essential difference within this scheme between disabled and non-disabled characters and subjects is that (initially, at least) the non-disabled characters take longer to meet their doom (for example, Oedipus) and their flaw becomes apparent only after a journey (the narrative) in which, Boal would argue, they have challenged the metaphorical state or order (represented as nature) in some way. Disabled characters are not assumed to have the power to challenge the order on a material level and therefore become objects of audience cartharsis far earlier in the story. Oedipus blinds himself near the very end of the story. His disablement does not present terror to the audience because it is the price paid for his (initially innocent) incest with his mother. Richard III, however, reveals his conscious nastiness in the first speech of the first act. The coercion of the audience is therefore encouraged by Richard's conscious setting of the anti-self agenda. The empathy with the 'tragedy' of *Richard III* is that he has made the audience hate disablement both personally and socially.

> Deform'd, unfinish'd, sent before my time
> Into this breathing world scarce half made up
> And that so lamely and unfashionable
> That dogs bark at me as I halt by them –

> Why, I, in this weak piping time of peace,
> Have no delight to pass away the time
> Unless to spy my shadow in the sun
> And descant on mine own deformity.[31]

For the audience, after this speech, he cannot do anything else but decline and eventually die. He is the embodiment of their repressed fears for their own fragile 'able-bodied' state. He tells us that he has 'no delight' in the time of peace (i.e. without war). However, his real battle is not the one he will fight with Richmond but 'the struggle' between his ego and the limitations imposed by his impairment. The general spuriousness of 'able-bodiment' – the fundamental lack of body-ownership – is transferred on to the character who appears conscious of his lack of body-ownership. The audience empathise with him as an object of the transference of this fear. The cathartic effect is in his willingness to play the oracle of hell. He does not even have the privilege of an ascendancy (like most tragic heroes) before a decline because there is no hope in disablement. *Disability tragedy, then, enters complete.* If, as Boal asserted, the flaw in the character is the site of the social, ethical, legal and moral order of the day *and* the price of transgressing these codes, then clearly disablement becomes the highest (that is, lowest) form of transgression. It is the final damnation. Take any example: the non-disabled hero of most plays sets out brave and ends up fallen and possibly redeemed, whereas disabled people set out fallen, possibly end up brave but are never redeemed! Tragic theatre is essentially similar to tragic charity advertising, the tragic medical model and the almost entire gambit of the tragic portrayal of disabled people in theatre, cinema, television, literature, photography and the like. The constructions of tragedy are the same, but only in the theories of radical theatre is the process laid out so clearly. This is because, unlike every other cultural form, drama and theatre have a ready-made 'laboratory' environment due to the proximity of the audience to the representation, the consumer to the product.

Brecht began the modern political consideration of the structured presence of the (un)consciousness of the audience *within* the text or presentation of the play itself.[32]

Again, this rejects the Aristotelian coercive system of *tragedy* through which, while the play exists in the light, the audience exists in the dark, experiencing the play as an object of catharsis and empathy. The purging of the emotions through empathy created an essentially hypnotic and uncritical relationship between the actors and the audience. They are separated as night is to day.

It was to disrupt this that Brecht developed process theatre in which the *Verfremdung*, the alienation device, became prominent: slogans on placards; living subtitles; lighting rigs exposed to the audience; an almost Shakespearean breaking of the text with addresses to the audience; the actors and audience in similar lighting; changing the tenses and delivery from actor-as-character to actor-as-narrator of same character; and so on. Borrowing from popular culture, he insisted that the story, the fable, must be established in the text of the play *and* in the production. Brecht called this 'epic' theatre which meant, in the Aristotelian sense, that the narrative had a timeless, universal principle within it. Brecht adapted this term to mean 'a sequence of incidents or events, narrated without artificial restrictions as to time, place or relevance to a formal "plot"'.[33]

These devices were used in such a way that the entire process of the play and the production encouraged fully conscious participation. As Brecht put it, 'the process of showing must also be shown.'[34] The actor was not an illusionist but someone who stood between the text and the audience. The relationships between these three stages – text, actor and audience – was dialectical and critical. Although never a member of the Party, Brecht's theatrical position was that of a communist critic of capitalism. This he saw as creating individuals and peoples whose lives and identities had become a brittle amalgam of seemingly coherent but ultimately fragmented pieces. Entertainment in traditional theatre attempted to pacify the viewer into accepting an illusion of coherence which, in fact, did not exist. Brecht's *V-Efekt* was to place the fragments in a context to arouse the viewers' powers of action, not to annul them. This is the essential difference between the passivity within the *tragedy* of the Aristotelian ideal in theatre, and the activity within the *mobilisation* of the Brechtian aesthetic.

The co-development, the intertwining, of the politics of the production with the politics of consumption in theatre has produced a 'post-Brechtian' movement, ranging from the absurdists,[35] to the American alternative theatre,[36] to the Theatre of Images,[37] to Gay Sweatshop and the left theatres of Britain, and which is linked by one essential current. This current is the rejection of the *tragedy principle* in representation *in the process* of countermobilised representation. However, the rejection is not simply at the level of veto – the yes/no, approval/disapproval inherent in an 'ethics' position – but is at the level of *process* and *product*. The inseperability of the two has been brought out into the open. Furthermore, radical drama is characterised by the development of a representation first from the position of those observed, and then from the position of those observing. The control of the image, then, is inherently in favour of those inhabiting it. As I said previously, these three tenets should create the anchors of radical disability photography. Indeed, Boal concluded his analysis of the tragic theatre thus:

> Aristotle's coercive system of tragedy survives to this day, thanks to its great efficacy. It is, in effect, a powerful system of intimidation. The structure of the system may vary in a thousand ways, making it difficult at times to find all the elements of its structure, but the system will nevertheless be there, working to carry out its basic task: the purgation of all antisocial elements. Precisely for that reason, the system cannot be utilized by revolutionary groups *during* revolutionary periods. That is, while the social ethos is not clearly defined, the tragic scheme cannot be used, for the simple reason that the character's ethos will not find a clear social ethos that it can confront. The coercive system of tragedy can be used before or after the revolution . . . but never during it![38]

Given that we are indeed living through a revolutionary period in terms of disability, we are in a position to develop a new laboratory process of disability imagery with wider references than has hitherto existed. The objection will be raised, of course, that in concentrating our energies into disability imagery *processes linked to product*, we may be making a kind of designer ghetto for ourselves. People may even say that we are retreating from the key sites of struggle, charity advertising in particular, and that we need to attack these sites first. Undoubtedly, there are many sites of struggle if we are to change the photographic representation of disabled people. However, the key site of representation development for disabled people intent on creating a disability photographic aesthetic has to be within a process-based laboratory of image-making: the proverbial workshop. (By 'workshop' I mean an agreed space, time and purpose reached by those within a particular process at any one time.) If we do not develop our own disability image-making processes, we will indeed be tilting at windmills. We will be the people interpreting oppressive imagery but not the people changing it.

It is here that we can pull radical drama theory and practice through the optics of the camera and back into the photographic process, while maintaining the radical possibilities for the subject. To be able to do this depends primarily on the existence of a 'workshop' photographic process, since much photography, for example reportage, does not generally exist in conditions of mutual agendas between observer and observed, between photographer and subject. We need to create a laboratory of the subject based on the dual identification of purpose, even the interchangeability, between the observer and the observed.

When I have run workshops with disabled people working on self- and social-representation, one thing has consistently struck me. This is the essential passivity of the participants in front of the camera. Of course, this is not peculiar to disabled people. The camera is the great documenter of the 'official' history of families, children, parents, holidays, schooldays, medical history, injury, slums and so on.[39] The movement of all things is frozen into one thing and one ideology. Prince Charles must be shown taller than Lady Di, although he's a good 6 inches shorter. He colludes because he has power – which the camera is about not only to compound but exaggerate – while others collude because they have no power. This collusion is like a religion, where the unnamed forces are greater than all mortals. This passivity, this frozen capitulation to the camera and an unfocused self-oppression is more so for disabled people (for the reasons I have outlined in previous chapters). It works because at the point when the subject, those photographed, are having the camera pointed at them and the 125th-of-a-second shutter is about to click, they must focus themselves as a vessel of signs from larger discourses which they may understand but do not control. Their life expectancy is summed up for the camera.

In this way, I have witnessed vibrant, hilarious, anarchic, politicised disabled people prepare to silence their body for the camera. Where their head was previously held up, it will start to dip. Their body language begins to freeze. Where once was a personal coherence is now the feeling of shifting sands. A hint of pulling back, of resistance to the negative synthesis that the camera is about to produce, will show in their eyes. They do not know the purpose of the image. They appear to know, they have been told that such-and-such an organisation is 'positive' about disability and that the organisation wants to prove it. Many disabled people are prepared to support this need but the demand (which is how a 'request' from those with power to those with less power often reads) can induce a sense of succumbing, of being press-ganged, rather than of free-giving or even celebratory-giving. To return to Boal's analysis of the role of the 'flaw', the basis of this unease is in the fact that the disabled subject is not aware of what symbolism, what social order, what transgressional value, is to be read into the image of their impairment or their disability.

There is little in photographic theory that will show the subject a different course of entry into the image. Indeed, it appears in photography that the best 'moments' are those 'captured' unawares. Countless magazines and newspapers show that the photographer's 'art' is to capture moments of beauty, pity, tragedy, despair, famine, dependency and so on, in that 'decisive moment' of visual poetics. Like the purpose of tragic theatre, these photographs also serve as objects for empathy and catharsis. The subject is shown but the process of showing is not. The body of the subject is a vehicle for the illumination of the photographer's (or, more correctly, the commissioner's) agenda. It is their reading which is paramount. Because nothing is built into the process of image-making to interrupt this *before the optics*, nothing within the image is likely to interrupt it *after the optics*.[40] There will be no *Verfremdung*. Therefore, despite the important resources of montaging, graphics, subtitling and so on, the image itself will not show processes or images of empowerment but images and processes of *disempowerment*. Without an alienation device, it will simply show alienation.

This has to be changed. The process of the articulation of power *by the subject* begins in the workshop because the context assumes a quantifiable time basis, whereas 'the shoot' does not. The process must begin from the consciousness of the subject, not from that of the photographer. However, it may not be clear to the subject that they possess such consciousness. Oppressed people's culture is always undervalued and misrepresented by the dominant culture. This devaluing of disabled people and disability culture can work its way through to the sense of self of disabled people. They can internalise negativity. It is not difficult to see why, if society within 'phase two' has no use-value attached to disabled people, some describe themselves as 'useless', and so on.

The first move in a counter-imagery workshop[41] then is not to present a *positive* challenge to this negative oppression but to site the negative 'useless' oppression itself. Charity advertising is the first part of the workshop process, not just because it is the most widespread form of the representational oppression of disabled people, but because it attempts to put the disabled people 'in their place'. It is when this place is named that the revolt begins. In viewing charity advertising in the workshop, disabled people confront these Mephisthophelean nightmares not as their own nightmares (since no disabled person I have ever met actually *made* a charity poster), but as the nightmare transference of non-disabled people. The flipchart is up and on to it go words like 'negative', 'dependent', 'fear inducing', 'black-and-white', 'cripples', and 'useless'. The charity posters become the screen on to which is thrown back in anger the bile they produce/induce.

The second move is to examine the relationship between the photograph (i.e. that which is photographed) and the charity. It becomes clear in this process that the names of the 'disability' charities are not in fact based on disability at all, but on impairment. They are not called 'The Inaccessible Stairs Charity', or 'The 50 per cent Unemployment Among People With Epilepsy Is Wrong Charity', they are called the

Spastics, Multiple Sclerosis, Epilepsy, etc. societies or charities. The separation of impairment from charity within the workshop introduces the group to each other on a profound level of disability identity, because it is here that the people can see their disabled communality, not their impairment difference. Since the name and purpose of the charity will be on the poster somewhere, this also introduces the issue of the relationship between image and text. People begin to explore what these two forms do to each other: how they control each other; how the image performs one job and the text another. The *packaging* of the oppressive image of the disabled person is also then seen as oppressive.

The third move is to enact the oppressive image. As written text, this appears cold, even vaguely dangerous. I would argue, however, that it is not something that can be prescribed (or proscribed for that matter), it is inevitable. Charity advertising is the dominant photographic form of reference for disabled people working with representation, and while it is not 'reclaimable', it is a necessary site of struggle *from the inside* as well as the outside. That is to say, it is my experience that disabled people will finally shatter these versions of themselves by critically inhabiting them. This process will also clear out from their psyches the oppressive museum of identities which they may have internalised. This is a process of private-production which, I would argue, is necessary before people can occupy, in safety, positions of public production and consumption images done by them or in their name. I am not advocating that disabled people emulate precisely the image they see on a charity ad, but that by going into character they will inevitably hijack it and fragment it.

The fourth move is to reintroduce text *within the image*. The control of the image's meaning through narrative text within charity advertising has become apparent. This allows the image, and the subject, to break up the responsibility of both image and text to tell the story. The point of this move is that it begins to position the image-story *off* the body and the impairment, which has hitherto been used as the 'natural' site of the message. This constructs at least two meanings in the photograph, that of image and that of text. It is in this dialogue that a separation of the different identities either forced upon or desired by disabled people can be enacted. The text might, for example, carry the story of a particular person's disablement history, whereas the photograph might visualise an alternative existence.

The fifth move is technical. The breaking-up of charity imagery from within will not occur unless the people witness the process. It is here that Polaroid is important. Basic Polaroid cameras can be adapted to be used with wheelchairs, and so on.[42] The Polaroid speed allows the subjects to travel through both observer and observed into self-observer. Each person can photograph, say, the person on their left, while this person will photograph them back. The camera is reversed and the same process reshot. Two Polaroids exist which narrate two people's constructions. The same process is repeated but this time the subject, the observed, directs according to references on the Polaroid which are or are not desired. This direction would include focusing, editing the body in or out of the frame, the camera direction in relation to the body, and so on. Clearly, it might be the facilitator's job to make these critical tools available or to use aural description, for example, if necessary. It is here, too, that the text might be further changed or redefined.

It is my experience that, at this stage, people who entered charity advertising in parody have by now completely rewritten it. The activity of the subject in the process is indivisible from the objective aims of the process. The one person observes and is observed within each Polaroid (refined more than the previous one, and so on). The Polaroids create a sequence, a narrative of empowerment. The Polaroid is the audience, the consumer, working almost simultaneously with the subject, the producer. The actor has become observer, the observer has become the actor. In the roles becoming interchangeable, the disabled person is breaking the cracked mirror of either/or representation. The narrative, however, is still likely to be focused on the body.

The power over the final image/narrative which Polaroid gives to the subject (within the safe environment) has to be reflected back to the user in order to go beyond the body (and the impairment) as the map of disablement. They have entered the coldest area, which is to put the body in the picture without any form of control. Charity advertising shows the disabled body as the collision between impairment and destiny, that is, fate. The destruction of this tragedy principle shifts the power back to the subject who has chosen to inhabit it in order to destroy it. The very act of recording this process breaks up the passivity inherent in a portrayal in which the subject cannot input or direct. The very deep-rooted 'tragedy' of oppressive disability representation has started to crack.

The Polaroid camera has become a marker-machine for stages in identity formation. The Polaroid imagery of the previous moves begins to saturate and exhaust the possibilities within the image-text mock charity arrangements. As the text shifts, the social acting to accompany it by the subject-director shifts. The images metamorphose away from charity advertising without any specific visual declarations of 'negative' or 'positive' imagery as such. The process of occupation of oppressive charity imagery by disabled people is crucial because of the inherent contradiction between the consciousness of the (disabled) actor of the self and the lack of consciousness portrayed in *all* charity advertising. The conscious Polaroid choice process jars with the notions of dependency which are being enacted within tragic imagery. This creates mini-*Verfremdungs*, little alienation devices, as this alchemy becomes celebrated. The process shows the shedding of a visual skin, namely the oppressive imagery of charity advertising (and, I repeat, this is by far the most prevalent form of regular disability/impairment imagery), which by implication denotes total dependency. The text which is being used to anchor the image-meaning and take the responsibility for meaning away from the body of the disabled person.

The sixth move, then, is to travel off the body. The medical model or social model would have been discussed in time before the practice and would have been examined and re-examined throughout the Polaroid process. The Polaroid has established the subject in the positions of both audience and player. The tragedy principle of most disability imagery has been broken by the process work because the person is mapping themselves not into a 'tragic' decline or position, but out of one. Their 'flaw' has been reclaimed and its meaning redefined. The possibilities of the projection on to the 'flaw', that is the impairment, are shifted away from non-disabled transference and on to disabled self-empowerment. These new meanings are in turn anchored by the text. Again, I am not describing a prescriptive stage. I believe these stages are the 'natural' processes (given how the workshop is set up in the first place, i.e. disabled-only, and so on) of shedding skins which automatically come about within the discourses of the oppressive social relations of phase two.

The seventh move, then, would be to record in Polaroid narrative the interface between the person and their space or non-space. The camera becomes a tool to record the interface between impairment and disablement: the wheel of their wheelchair against the first step of stairs; the gawking of schoolchildren; the lean-over of patronising men and women; the lighting which causes seizures or migraine; the rejection letter of the job application; and so on. This can be enacted either naturalistically or in a constructed situation (or, of course, in both ways).

The Polaroid narrative would record the clash, the paradox, the *struggle* between the person with the impairment and their disabling environment. Here is positive imagery because it names the struggle. It does not, however, in the manner of standard left reportage, name the struggle solely of the observed. The process has created the conditions for the interchangeability of observer with observed. The actor has become audience and the audience actor. The seventh move would end with the resynthesis of the first process, the siting of the body from fragments of identity, with the second process of siting the body in external struggle, into a tableau of the self. This final tableau might be anchored by a final text or banner piece. The materials then exist to transform this work into any scale. If the Polaroid were type 55 (i.e. 4″ × 5″ negative size) or type 665 (which produces a medium format negative plus positive), then these of course could be printed up, or if not, they could be enlarged with a colour photocopier. (Finkelstein has argued that it is the new technologies which are precipitating a shift from 'phase two' to 'phase three'. Certainly, in my work I am exploring the narrative limits of photographic technologies with the political expansion of the disability movement.)

The camera has now turned. Disabled people, like black people/people of colour, women, and so on, are aware that their bodies are constructed as the site of oppression. It is unavoidable, therefore, that, in the first instance at least, the body is a site of struggle. As I said in Chapter 1, the change from 'phase-two' notions to 'phase-three' notions is more than a simple adoption of one abstraction for another. The successful adoption of one for another is rooted in its relevance to lived experience. In my experience of being a disability photographer, disabled people need space to tell the story, the journey, of their body and in doing so, reclaim and be proud of themselves. What is needed, again, are *processes of image mapping and subject/object interaction* to carry this self-love into mobilised action at the point of oppression; that is, access.[43] However, Marx said that nature's only law is labour. By this he meant *to process*. A radical disability photographic practice will portray the process of self-love, the process of personal power and the process of political power.

The moves that I have so far described are a suggestion for that process. In other words, the image identification of impairment which began with charity advertising has to be dealt with *subjectively* before we can proceed to other forms of *disability* imagery. I am aware that I am greatly simplifying the process. Obviously, there are any number of levels of anger and pain, ranging from straightforward access issues to the repressed memory of disabled incest survivors. However, the process of the theatre of the self in Polaroid mapping (or even without Polaroid) with one's own scripto-visual/auto-visual text/imagery is still essentially the same, at least in terms of photographic representation.

There is no such thing as memory without representation or fantasy, and therefore there can be no such thing as radical disability photography without that which allows the reality-fantasy duality of process to exist. I don't mean this, for example, as Freud meant it in his suppression and diversion of incest pain into 'fantasy projection', but in the sense that the imagination's relationship to memory cannot be separated into single categories of objective reality and subjective fantasy. A truly radical disability imagery must admit a panorama of experience, life and action. However, there are signs of a 'positivist' morality seeping into the issue of disability imagery. In this world, the issue is separated into a simple negative/positive divide, for instance, a smile is positive, a frown is negative. Of course, there is some call for this since it is undeniable how oppressive most disability imagery is. However, my argument is that the *permanent* route out of oppressive imagery begins with its dismantling by caricature within the processes of a workshop schema, as I have suggested above. Of course, this is only the beginning of the process of dismantling oppressive disability imagery.

The purpose of this transformation is to prevent the development of a 'positive' disability imagery that suppresses the past and the oppression. A 'positive' disability imagery which does so is on the horizon and has to be confronted. (One only has to witness the 'positive' use of disabled people in commercial advertising in the US – for instance in the McDonald's advertisements – to see how the cleanliness of positivity is being worked to hide the dirt of oppression.)

A truly empowering 'school' of positive disability imagery must contain the signs of the pain, the sign of the reclamation of the body, the revisualising of the 'flaw' of the impairment, the marks of struggle and overcoming, and signs for a future. Access and representation are the goals but fantasy and reality, subjectivity and objectivity must all play their part in the naming of a disability image identity. The process of showing must also be shown. All political movements contain radical and reformist elements. They are parodied as 'left' and 'right' but they are often issues of tactics and timing. However, one thing is clear. The indivisibility between process and product must continually be reiterated. The presence of the power and information discourses surrounding the dominant forms of disability/impairment imagery will be revealed by an analysis of the process by which the representations have been made. Photography is drama, not reality. Its powers of political realism lie within its critical engagement of its discursive context. This is its task. The reality principle of imagery cannot be assumed naturally. The ability of an image to impart the reality of a political struggle (in our case, the disability movement's struggle for access and representation) is within the image's ability to force a collision between the old consciousness and the new, between the old discourses and the new. We do have to pressure all aspects of oppressive image-makers to get their 'act' sorted out, but the core site of change is within ourselves and our own processes. If we can develop these, the non-disabled mountain will indeed come to our disabled Mohammed.

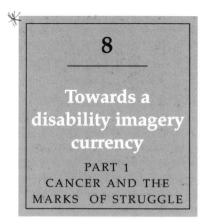

8

Towards a disability imagery currency

PART 1
CANCER AND THE
MARKS OF STRUGGLE

David Hevey Can you elaborate on how getting ill made you value political and practical photographic theory?

Jo Spence I think it was when I was ill that I understood for the first time what it was to be a victim. Previously, all the theory I learnt was head stuff. When I was ill, I suddenly realised that, in reading discourse theory, I was in a discourse, a medical discourse, and I hadn't understood what a discourse was before.

Here I was on the production line, as the kind of fodder passing along between doctors and consultants. That was the beginning of it. I began to see how they constructed a world view through the way they worked and what I wanted was irrelevant really. I was the patient, who had to be managed, got better, but I didn't exist, other than what their discourse made me. They didn't want to know anything about me really, apart from 'where is it and how soon can we take it off?' The process of theory taught me how to research, and the substance gave me critical tools.

I think coming from my working-class background, I was frightened of everything that had a vague look of an institution about it. I suddenly realised that I actually knew how to use a library. I knew how to get information. So the second level of using theory was to actually begin to find out what I could do to help myself and that threw me into the middle of 'what is knowledge?' And 'where does knowledge come from?'

Having been diagnosed, I abandoned what I thought I knew, which was a series of stereotypes about cancer. I'd only experienced them through other people and it was something I couldn't bear to think about, really, because my mother had died of it and all I could remember was a series of silences and around the silence was terror for me. A no-go area. Don't think about it, you're safer that way.

I literally had to plunge into the abyss and find out what I could about what they were doing to me, or what they wanted me to do. My mother was working class and didn't ever question what happened to her as a cancer patient and the motto I had in the family, in relation to health in particular, was 'Do as you're told'. The medical profession is God, yet in my family, the doctors never delivered the goods. No one ever got better of anything. They just got steadily worse. It wasn't acknowledged like that, because, like many 'non-disabled people', they were held in check by drugging; this is how the bronchitis, depression, arthritis and so on were 'dealt with'.

D.H.   And was the bottom line self-blame?

J.S.   Yes. I think I grew up with the idea that disablement or illness was inevitable, that drugging was inevitable and that maybe being locked up or cut open was inevitable. A part of me was so terrified, that I didn't have anything to lose when my turn came, which is why I refused what they wanted to do to me. I refused to have a mastectomy and I see now in terms of theory, that I was stage-managed at various points on the production line, into trying to turn me into a well-behaved patient by traumatising me by saying 'If you don't do what we tell you . . .' or 'You're being very naughty' or 'You're being hysterical', or 'We haven't got time to deal with all these questions, we'd never get round', and so on.

D.H.   The passive lump?

J.S.   Exactly. It was like an obstacle race. I got past the consultant and went back to my GP and she immediately said, 'You've been very naughty, you've got to have your breast removed, never mind what you found here and there, I am going to send you back to someone in London who'll take it off.' The fact that I had adopted an alternative approach via traditional Chinese medicine was brushed aside as irrelevant. Toxic drugs can't cure anything really, they just hold things in check. The point is you need to *appear* to get better. And to all intents and purposes from capitalism's point of view you do get better, back on your feet, back to work and off the sick.

I think what is quite interesting about my work is that I was non-disabled, then became disabled, and I operate at these borders. So my work is very much about person-centred, holistic health.

D.H.   You have said that your family moved in and out of illness: did this give you the position to turn breast cancer and person-centred health issues into political photography? Does the growing up on fragile ice create, if you like, metaphorical value in your cancer work? Can it speak other languages?

J.S.   That's interesting. I think at the point where I was struggling to understand what I could do to help myself, I certainly wasn't aware of anything called patient-centred medicine at that point, or group-activity in relation to health. It wasn't until much later that I saw it metaphorically. What happened was that I did the work and received not a word from anybody about it. It was like it fell into the greatest silence I have ever come across. So, I did what I learnt to do as a working-class woman, which was to justify why I did my work by saying, well of course it is a metaphor for all kinds of struggle, and of course it is, but actually the original reason wasn't that at all.

The more I said it, the more I believed it. But I can't tell you what it felt like, first of all having cancer, secondly trying to talk about it, and being continually asked, 'Well, how are you Jo?' and you'd see their eyes glaze over and they'd think, 'Christ, I hope she's not going to tell me!' The reception of the work was amazing; that is, an amazing silence! I went to this gallery opening of my work and there was silence except for someone coming up and saying 'I like the green card it's on'!

D.H.   Listening to what you're saying, all the areas you identify – education, the polytechnic, the reception at the opening, the medical profession – are these areas where the politics of the body are dealt with on an intellectual rather than an experiential level?

J.S.   Yes. For people experiencing impairment first-hand, it is a struggle both to maintain our bodies and get the struggle heard. Firstly, they are shit-scared of all forms of actual production. From factory production to the production and re-production of illness. Ironically, I would argue cynically, the only way I could become acceptable was to turn my illness into a piece of work at one level.

D.H.   Some sort of abstraction?

J.S.   Yes. So that it could be handled by abstract people. When the work goes to places where people have cancer, there's no taboo at all, they just fall about you with open arms and say, 'How marvellous to be able to talk about it. That we could talk about having a breast removed or being badly damaged by surgery or our hair dropping out or whatever.' So, it's the difference between audiences: if you put it into one context it's bad art, you put it into another context, it's brilliant information.

D.H.   But it has shifted the radical photography base quite seriously. So, as you say in a lot of your articles, it's social-sciences, teachers, users, actual utility users that love the work, whereas the photographic intelligentsia or the 'counter-culturalists' have found it, in a perverse way, *too* usable and *too* located.

J.S.   Oh, they think it's a bit low brow and they can't talk about it and, as you say, they're not in their bodies. I talk about a textual body, and then I talk about a body that I inhabit and so many male bastions and institutions don't want that. They don't know what to do because they're so used to the female nude; that's *The* body!

D.H.   That whole absenting of body *as a site of struggle* does meet its final nemesis within disability and the access issue. Images of disabled people, particularly those used by charity advertising, have constructed disabled people as the refuse of the social body.

J.S.   Yes, that's right, and the breakdown of the body and the potential for death, that's the point isn't it? I am presenting a supposed 'hidden' disability and the marks of struggle against the medical or cultural discourses. I think that people live in such a world of fantasy around what they think is going on and kidding themselves that they have some 'control', that a kind of chink in the armour like that is terrifying.

That's without all the other things that are going on. But I think cancer is a particular taboo because with cancer you could end up losing a leg, an eye quite suddenly, or a breast. It's an illness that is unpredictable. It does have different characteristics from other more fixed medical conditions, such as cerebral palsy. With cancer, what I've known is people gradually having bits of them taken away until their bowels are not working any more and they can't breathe and so on and so on. And they still appear to be 'normal'.

D.H.   They still have the temptation to 'pass' within that because of the pressure.

J.S.   When someone who has cancer is finally dying, that's one thing, but many families go into mourning at the first diagnosis as a form of disavowing their own pain and fears. On the other hand, what you'll get is this continual lying going on about kidding everybody that everything's better than it is and, of course, the eternal gratitude.

They're encouraged to because people can't stand it. For instance, going back to my father. He was a 'chest case' for years and when I look back at the photographs of him he's always trying to look normal but actually his face is pained from trying to breathe. And whenever he was with people, he mustered his energies together to appear to be 'normal'. But if you saw him running for the bus, he would go blue in the face and collapse on to the bus. If he had to go upstairs, that would be it, because of the smoke. People wouldn't see that.

D.H.   And no criticism of the drugs or medical regime because they're too frightened.

J.S.   And grateful to have the treatment. What you're dealing with is, if you're involved in any sort of 'against-the-grain' work on something like cancer, is the stereotyped notion of knowledge. You're up against the power relationship that each patient is caught up in with their consultant. And they say 'my consultant'. It's like a hang-over from the Royal Doctor.

I think, to come back to 'where does knowledge come from?', just how can you produce work that actually counters that weight of belief in the invincibility of people who are patently failing in front of your eyes! Some cancers are now curable, but most of them aren't. But 90 per cent of them could be prevented actually if we had better working and environmental conditions or weren't so stressed and needed to smoke and drink to kill the pain of daily life.

When I was ill and was told I would have to go on a diet for the rest of my life, I felt totally deprived that I wasn't going to be able to eat junk food any more. Then, when I started to get into it I felt kind of holy, y'know, 'I'm eating this good food', but behind that was the desire continually to revert to eating junk food (and I do) because I am emotionally dependent on it.

And the worse the problem with cancer got, the more I wanted to eat. I went to a holistic conference and asked the question 'Given that we see diet and food intake as the primary question, how do you tackle the problem of emotional eating?' Which is what the whole culture is caught up with.

D.H.   And what was their answer?

J.S.   They hadn't got one, beyond saying you have to take a more holistic attitude, but what does that mean?

D.H.   Photography as a process necessarily admits consumerism and rapid production, but you've brought in issues of class- and body-language. The vulgar physical body occupying the pure cerebral theoretical body. In this sense, not only do you not 'behave yourself' medically, you don't behave yourself culturally or intellectually. Would you agree?

J.S.   Yes, I would. What I've been through is most extraordinary, I couldn't call it crucifixion exactly, because I'm not religious, but I actually thought I was doing quite radical work and it has never been named as such.

Then what happened was the AIDS crisis became apparent at the point where I was ill and, suddenly, all these people that were right-on theoreticians were suddenly all going on about AIDS. Now, that's not to denigrate that issue. Simon Watney, in particular I wouldn't wish to denigrate, but clearly other people have jumped into the AIDS industry. My answer to that is go and make a project out of the politics of your own life!

To me, the struggle is between anger and ultra-silence and I actually can deal with anger better than ultra-silence. Coming from my background, ultra-silence means I don't exist. There's no position to speak from.

But let me give you the peak of my experience as a cancer patient. I went to the third National Conference of Self-Help Groups. I took my Picture of Health exhibition by invitation and put it up. And I did a workshop on images of cancer and disability. A lot of people came to my workshop and said, 'Oh yes, it's very interesting but I don't know what to do with it. Y'know, I can't deal with things ideologically, I am only here for practical information.' And then, when I was taking the exhibition down, a couple of women helped me and they said, 'Why are you so angry, dear?' And I said, 'Well, don't you think there's a lot to be angry about?' And they said, 'But they're doing the best they can.' And I realised what was happening. At the conference, in the final plenary session, what was emerging was that the whole conference was virtually treating itself like handmaidens to the medical profession. There were only a couple of critically dissenting voices.

But all the radical social workers who were there on a political and class base were asking the most difficult questions I have ever heard, saying 'We're not here to service the medical profession. We actually want to discuss the politics of illness.'

And I was trying to ask another sort of question which was, 'How is our illness represented and how does that help to position us through our basic ignorance? Of course, that was another set of shushes.

D.H.   To question the very basis of the welfare state medicine, which is based on non-holistic, toxic intervention, is still seen as the ultimate transgression. In the left, one is seen as a traitor if you criticise the medical regime. Not only are you anti-Tory, you're anti-Labour!

J.S.   That's right. They can't get their head round the notion of patient-centred medicine, basically. The only place I ever heard what I would call politics was at the British Holistic Medical Association which is the rival to the British Medical Association.

They actually tried to have a structure for the organisation that had doctors, nurses, alternative healers and patients with parity at the organisational level, but they kept the front up that it was run by doctors, because that way they would be acknowledged within the discourses of medicine as having equal power to argue. But it was actually about patient-centred medicine. But they did talk about how, if you have a holistic attitude to someone, you have to take account of their social and environmental factors which would take them perhaps into green politics. These are medical people talking, they're not saying, fill the buggers up with drugs and let's get on with it, let's have the next patient.

But bringing this back to my work, I see myself as good old anarchist Spence, blundering around between the different discourses between cultural politics and alternative health and mainline health and actually being silenced at every count. Except that privately I was lauded quite a lot and told, 'Oh that's good, keep going into the hospitals and doing that', but people couldn't acknowledge it in public because their jobs would be on the line. The work does help create a climate, but it's about the most lonely thing I have ever been involved in, in my entire life.

But, essentially, my relationship to theory is a very practical one. I'm not interested in abstractions, I'm interested in how you can use theory and who it's for and for what purpose. I can't assume from my background that I can trust all theories any more than all accountants or all lawyers.

D.H.   It seems to me that your work does reside right in those discourses but, as an aesthetic, it seems to me to talk about a spiritual vacuum with consumerism and the commodity. Unlike practically all other discourse theory, the site of your theory is actually in the plastic commodity. You seem to reinhabit a popular form, the family album, and bring to it a militant anarchy it wouldn't appear to possess.

J.S.   Yes, but I think my work will endure because it's actually funny. I want it on the biting edge between 'Isn't it hysterically funny?' and 'Isn't it absolutely unbearably awful?' It's the working-class ploy, or disabled ploy, that you joke about adversity. When I was in hospital, one of the things I said to Terry was: 'If they want my breast, I'm gonna ask for it back in a jar!'

So my work deals with many forms, including self-analysis, inhabiting the centre of the web, inhabiting the theories, but also populism and our own catharsis with vulgarity and getting rid of our shame. But it's not just getting rid of it, it's enjoying it and sharing it. It's a mix between discourse theory and the seaside postcard! Also, I produce and operate in a place and time-zone that colleges, institutions and so on don't. They are into philosophical time, producing work once a year or less. Radical intervention demands a bit more than that, I think.

D.H.   Which also, of course, ties up with the propagandist.

J.S.   Well, the thing is that my work moves right across that because I work with what is seen as 'negative' imagery. And in coming to terms with the negative, the so-called negative, all those images become part of my dialectical way of thinking about myself. That which is hidden away, the shadow, is out in the open!

In phototherapy, I tend to work with clients who've heard me talk or seen my work, so they know my agenda. The first thing that has to be established between us is that there is no hierarchy. Second, that I am not in a position of knowledge and I can't deliver some goods to them; that basically, I'm on a journey and I will share the techniques I'm learning for unpicking the threads of my life by becoming assertive and getting new knowledge *with* them. I don't want to be positioned as someone who they have to defer to. I also establish safety by showing I'm able to take a hell of a lot of flack and stress and if they go to pieces, I'll be there. But I want them to fight back all the time. In therapy, the whole thing is to facilitate the other person to feel safe enough to hear what *they've* got to say, and I'm the witness or advocate.

And I'll use any tools to do that, from playing games or getting them to draw their feelings, or setting them photo assignments or working on family album photographs or using masks or setting up psycho-dramatic tableaux with them. For example, working with someone who is an 'emotional eater', I created the family table and she played through all the parts round the table at childhood meal times to the camera. She said she had never realised what went on before as she went round and inhabited each seat and became the person. Then she could actually *see* what was going on in the family, which was that her mother was servicing her father, who just looked out of the window most of the time, psychically speaking, while the siblings got on with their rivalry. That's no big deal, but she'd found that out in about five minutes! She could've talked to me for ten years and still not come out with it.

So, it's the enactment or re-enactment of something and the making of the image which is taking them further and further into whatever they need to work on. I work with people on a one-to-one basis and the most I've ever done is ten sessions with anyone. And people become very assertive and self-knowledgeable and they're not into family blaming. They actually start to take responsibility for themselves and become empowered in some way. Some then begin to marry up this with their politics.

A lot of the people I work with initially have no sense of value of themselves at all, and therefore they sometimes treat other people like shit. And my job is not actually to punish them but to reflect back to them what they're doing. So somebody pisses me about, I reflect it back to them. I don't have a go at them.

D.H.   So you're working on a peer-group political model of photography and meaning?

J.S.   Yes that's right. I've also taken the therapy techniques I've known into women's groups and they've adopted methods of having a dialogue in the group and stuff shifted in the group like lightning. We no longer have long theoretical positions being set up, we actually weave in and out of public face, into private trauma, into theory, into therapy. As women, we're able to do that weaving and keep the ball afloat and we're learning to have a different sort of peer group.

D.H.   No longer just terrorist versus those brutalised?

J.S.   That's an extreme version of it, but yes. The fact of the matter is that a lot of people within political groups are disavowing their family patterns that they bring with them. My experience is that a lot of people on the left are actually in extreme distress from unresolved family traumas or interclass traumas, or the transition from non-disabled to disabled, and so on. I'm saying that there are different articulations of rebellion but people need to know how to rebel! As Terry Dennett says, the point is not just to be visible as a human being but to make the process visible.

Cancer has taught me that life isn't a dress rehearsal, this is it and you only get the one chance. And the problem is, having nearly died, I have to ration my energy so that I don't completely burn myself out again. On the other hand, I don't want to go and retire in the country and grow cabbages, in order to prolong my life!

This is my disability paradox. I will never be fit again. I have an impaired liver and blood, I have very bad lungs. Breast cancer was just the tip of the iceberg. As my body has been fragmented, so my disablement is fragmented.

I think it's important to understand that all my work is about demystification – both of the self and of the medical and family discourses which defined me for much of my life. I needed to find out who I had been told I was before I could contradict it. In that sense, the methods are tools which I share with the others. I use my own life history very much as a case study – not to privilege my chronic disability or my particular set of life events.

Notes to Plates 50–4

Jo Spence: Cancer and the marks of struggle

50   *How Do I Begin to Take Responsibility for my Body?*
A montage of photographs produced (at my instigation) by working with two different women. In the centre, we record part of my daily routine for self-help holistic medicine which includes pectoral muscle exercises. This is surrounded by images of body fragments which ask questions ('How do I begin to take responsibility for my body?') taken in an early phototherapy session. Phototherapy evolved between myself and Rosy Martin out of the use of techniques from a range of therapies, plus photographic skills. It is a form of re-enactment of repressed memories, a kind of photo-theatre, or psychic realism. The work was always reciprocal – I offered Rosy a session in return for doing a session with me, building on co-counselling skills. Although this was initially done as a form of self-healing, the work was later used in my exhibition The Picture of Health? in 1984. This questions the politics of cancer and is still used in health and educational venues.

51   *The Ritual of the Ward Rounds*
After years of being an agitprop photographer as part of the feminist left, then studying communication theory as a mature student, in 1982 I collapsed and was taken into hospital with breast cancer. Here for the first time I decided to use my snapshot camera to document what was going on around me, particularly the ritual of the ward rounds.

This picture was taken on the day of my diagnosis and the consultant and his student doctors are now two beds away from me. I noticed that the women in the next bed was reading *The Star* and included it in the picture. This is a form of constructed documentary which I later used to comment on the fact that the 'star' of the medical scenario is the consultant and not the patient. When the group got to my bed I stopped taking photographs out of sheer terror.

52   *Rite of Passage*

From a phototherapy session with Rosy Martin on powerlessness. I re-enact the moment of being marked up for amputation (against which I rebelled). This is part of a narrative fragment in which I told myself the story of my own infantilisation at the hands of the medical profession.

53   *Narratives of Dis-ease*

Done in one phototherapy session this booby prize image represents photographs from eight years of my life. This work is an example of the ways in which it is possible, through the process of phototherapy, to distil feelings/events/ideas into icons: these can then be made public in the hope of disorientating the viewers' expectations, prompting them to an interior dialogue with themselves. This stands in contradiction, or at least is complementary to, earlier work done for The Picture of Health?, which was an information exhibition. In future venues, the two pieces of work will be brought together in the same space.

Monster. In a phototherapy session some six years after the original event, I create an icon of how I felt I was treated when I spoke to people about my disability. By breaking the taboos which surround cancer I felt ostracised and in some ways made to bear the brunt of other people's fears and pain. Through confronting my own feelings about this in therapy I became much stronger and began to understand that I needed to work through my socially induced shame, learn to love myself . . . and leave others to deal with their own feelings. I could no longer be a whipping dog. At this point I was by now lecturing in hospitals about aesthetics and body fragmentation, and in arts and media courses about holistic health, power relationships and family albums. It was difficult to keep shifting the terms of the discourses I entered but each had its own specificity and I had to address that in order to be heard. These two images are part of an artwork called Narratives of Dis-ease which was part of the Great British Art Show in Glasgow in 1990. I felt it important to try to raise issues of representation and body politics within the space of galleries, as well as educational venues.

54   *Cultural Sniper*

In a phototherapy session with my partner David Roberts in which I am trying to ask myself who I am, I finally came up with the category which was missing from my work on health and disability . . . that of myself as a cultural sniper. This icon, of controlled anger, small ammunition aimed at specific targets, pleased me and allowed me a degree of healing as a disabled artist. It was recently used on the front cover of a radical arts magazine called *Variant*.

HOUSEHOLD HINTS FOR VISITORS

It is *okay to discuss* my health, leukaemia or cancer but ONLY if you respect the following guidelines:

1 That you *take seriously* my choices and attitude to my own condition.
2 That you *don't criticise* my choice of treatment, either directly or indirectly, from the point of view of your own ignorance or fears, thereby discounting the considerable amount of research I have undertaken over the years.
3 That you *don't discuss me* as if I am dying, killing myself, a victim, a burden, boring, unlovable, depressed, hopeless, guilty . . . (any of these might seem to be true at some time but I am making every effort to recover my full health, energy and spirit).
4 That you accept *my choice* not to take drugs or submit to surgery.
5 That you *don't off-load* anecdotes about other treatments and their success or failure unless I invite you to do so.
6 That you *don't tell me* about the last six illnesses your auntie had.
7 That you *understand* that being sick is not 'my own fault', that illness is not self-created.
8 That *my body* is not 'failing me'. (In many ways my body is my best friend.)
9 That it is *okay to be happy* about your own life and health. (I'll share your happiness.)
10 That you *remember* that David and I are a team . . . He is working quite hard towards my full recovery (as are a number of our close friends).
11 That *I am not* 'courageous' or 'inspiring' or 'brave' . . . looking after myself is a job to be done well with love for the self.

Jo Spence, February 1991

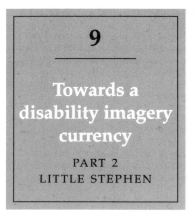

9

Towards a disability imagery currency

PART 2
LITTLE STEPHEN

INFANTILISM, PROJECTION AND NATURALISM IN THE CONSTRUCTION OF MENTAL DISABLEMENT
Jessica Evans

There are many ways of describing my brother. That he has Down's Syndrome is one fact about him and does not, to my mind, tell you very much. Sometimes I objectify him, by seeing him as someone 'with Down's Syndrome', someone who is 'different'. On the other hand, I just relate to him as my brother; I feel close to him, we have shared experiences and we have the same looks. But even as I write about him as an individual, I am doing so in the context of this book which brings us back to focusing on him as a member of a particular category. Does the reductive process begin as soon as I single him out as the subject of my text? Down's Syndrome is merely one fact about my brother and does not in any sense define his whole person.

If we consider that some of the people categorised as mentally handicapped have been incarcerated for life in 'sub-normality' hospitals (40,000 in 1983); were denied educational rights until 1970; have been educated after this date in segregated 'special' schools; that there has been no post-19 education provided; that job opportunities and independent living have been denied them; that dental and health care provision have been of low priority and ambivalently administered on the basis of assumptions about quality of life and vanity; that since June 1987 the legal precedent has been set to sterilise women without their consent and that this has happened in practice since then – then we can see that 'theirs' has been a history of oppression and exclusion by the institutions of medical science, the charities, education and the media industry.[1]

The 'treatment' of people with learning difficulties has often been justified by asserting the existence of an incurable and innately useless condition. Such is the supposed truth of the 'mentally handicapped' person. In this way, the 1985 Mencap poster, 'On Friday May 6th' proposes that potential is a matter of biological predisposition. In a paradoxical conflation of magic and science, these babies in this poster are pictured as literally stigmatised at birth, labelled by the medical profession, but as if their impairment were dealt with by an unseen hand of fate. Thus, 'the mentally handicapped' are held to be a homogeneous group of people who are more like one another than anyone else because of their shared nature; and therefore, whose situation, behaviour, actions and needs are simply expressions of a deeper biological primacy. Hence, are what in fact evaluative statements pass themselves off as biological facts.[2] For example, there is often an attempt to construct the congenital fact of Trisomy-21 (Down's Syndrome) as the underlying cause of all behaviour and ability of this 'group', so that actions and behaviour which may be contingent upon a wide range of social interactions and identities are always regarded as expressions of a diagnosed order. However, people designated as mentally handicapped also inhabit other social identities as classed, raced and gendered subjects, and are therefore stratified in relation to access to education, health care and political and policy-making agencies. While, for example, the medical diagnosis of Down's Syndrome can establish a link between the specific nature of the cell structure (Tri-21) and observable characteristics of the body, there is not a correlation between these signs and mental capacity and ability. Yet it is certain visual characteristics of the impairment in and on the body which are read as signs of mental disorder in both medical photography and charity posters as if there were a necessary relation between visual appearances and learning ability. *It is as if everything can be given to the gaze and known through it.*

It is crucial to understand that this is not just a question of semantics. That we can refer at all to a 'mentally handicapped' person simply indicates our acceptance of an already existing value system that classifies and demarcates difference – the divergence of an imaginary 'abnormality' from an imaginary 'normality'. This does not deny the real existence of people with particular needs. They may even be dependent, as we all are, upon a network of supportive structures. However, it can be shown historically that what has happened to this group is contingent upon certain economic and political factors within the specificity of western capitalism and its growth; a society which subordinates all value and all social life to a means-ends rationality.

The roots of the contemporary situation regarding 'mental handicap' can be found in the emergence of the notion of *population* at the beginning of the nineteenth century. What distinguished approaches to population, as Foucault has argued, was the development of new institutions and techniques of power designed to observe, monitor and intervene in all aspects of the phenomenon of population. The biological traits of a populace became relevant factors for economic management and it became necessary to organise around them an apparatus that would ensure the constant increase of their utility. The body now becomes the function of a utilitarian schema and, crucially, becomes the bearer of qualities of fertility, sickness, health, strength, and moral behaviour which were seen as vital to the future of the nation.[3]

Darwin had provided a theory emphasising the evolutionary effects at the level of population of individual variations. Eugenic theory, as a specific form of social Darwinism, assumed that the existing social hierarchy resulted from the differences in the innate qualities and capacities of individuals. Beginning in the late nineteenth century under the influence of social Darwinism and culminating in the mental-testing movement in the US and Nazi Germany, ideologists came to apply the term 'degeneration' to people whose mental and physical impairments were thought to be the outcome of hereditary factors. All those who could not fill a function useful to the productive needs of 'society' were constituted as a biological problem requiring a biological solution. The eugenic move was the linking of the notions of idiocy, disease, pauperism, 'the criminal mind', the poor and the sick, with notions of heredity. The sick must be segregated from the healthy and the rate of reproduction amongst the 'lower orders' must be reduced in order to avoid the degeneration of civilised stock.[4] The Mencap poster 'On Friday May 6th', therefore, can be understood in the context of the debate about the 'right to life' which emerged very publicly in the 1980s at the same time as the transition to community care.[5] Using the rhetoric of medical diagnosis, it evokes fear, as if 'mental handicap' is a hovering fear amongst

'Us'. Demonstrating that the eugenics discourse is alive and well, its subliminal message is that it would be better if certain people ceased to exist as they threaten our normal existence.

In 1896, the National Association for the Care and Control of the Feebleminded was set up in Britain. It functioned as a pressure group advocating the lifetime segregation of 'defectives'. The group's emphasis on the prevention of sexuality and reproduction was motivated by middle-class fears about working-class fertility. The fear of these 'animal' actions was in turn validated by Séguin, the nineteenth-century educationalist, whose views continued to set the agenda for the conception of disabled people living somewhere between an animal state and a possible humanity. This justified the improving of the 'treatment' of 'idiots' in terms of their possible transformation into more socially acceptable (i.e. productive) people, which was one of the main arguments of nineteenth-century reformers and beyond. The principle of moral treatment as opposed to the brute physical treatment of the eighteenth century was exemplified in Séguin's phrase: 'He will not but we will for him.' Charities originated from a perceived need to anaesthetise an ethically disturbing situation. The presence of large numbers of disabled people thus gave charities their *raison d'être* as organised assuagers of the bourgeois conscience.

The shift in charity advertising from 'fund raising' to 'attitude change' (see Chapters 3 and 4) has attempted to address the 'enlightened reformist' consciousness. People are asked to *see* and understand the 'handicapped person' as acceptable. This type of advertising is happening at a time when thousands of long-term residents are being released from large hospitals into local communities under government policies aimed at achieving public sector expenditure cuts. Of course, there is not necessarily a 'local community' to go to. Also, the intended 'integration' is viewed suspiciously by both sides of the disability paradox (see Chapter 2). While 'mental handicap' is constructed as 'other', and this 'other' appears to be a threat, then the non-disabled 'community' is likely to perceive the presence of people with learning disabilities as a threat.

But how does the photographic practice of 'mental handicap' charity advertising construct this form as a given category? To what extent is our idea of 'mental handicap' in fact a mental image, a representation? In a MORI poll conducted for Mencap in March 1982, 62 per cent thought 'mentally handicapped' people should be cared for in the community and 23 per cent thought they should be in segregated schools or hospitals. But there is a contradiction in the thinking of the samples – nearly half expressed considerable concern at having 'handicapped' people as neighbours and the vast majority of these were people who were not in contact with people with learning disabilities. Thus, it seems that even when people are in favour of dismantling institutional provision, the 'community' into which disabled people are meant to go is located 'somewhere else'. Here, 'the community', as an internal object in people's minds, operates as a metaphor for imprisonment.

Two years later, the headline for a 1984 Mencap poster presented us with the attitude of the prejudiced viewer which the photograph and the rest of the text are supposed to refute. 'No Sense, No Feelings?' is rebutted with 'They may not think as fast but they feel as deeply.' A man and a woman with their arms locked together in a heart shape are shown aspiring to an institution of culture (marriage). The reading of the image is rooted in standard wedding photography, but the effect of the poster is that of parody. The couple are isolated and seem to be emerging from a black background. They are photographed with a wide angled lens which, when used in close-up, projects lips, noses and hands into the viewer's space. The use of top lighting casts shadows into their eyes and under their chins and emphasises the creases in their dishevelled clothing. The effect is semi-Gothic. Furthermore, the man has a pocketful of combs implying an obsessional activity, but this is paradoxically offset by both their heads of hair being untidy and uncombed. The poster indicates that this is the 'handicapped character', who is slightly mad, certainly very peculiar, and who tries to pass as normal by aspiring to the honorific portrait and institution of marriage. In psychoanalytical terms, this is a construction of two people in a regressive state, as not having developed beyond the instinctual perversity of childhood. The text of the poster expresses similar sentiments to those of animal protectors, who refer to animals being unable to speak, think and intellectualise, but which feel

We wanted to produce images not as a means of establishing evidence about 'what mentally handicapped people are really like' but in order to politicise the concept of 'mental handicap'. Taking the form of a dramatic narrative sequence, the images question the involvement of various historical and contemporary institutions in the lives of people with learning disabilities and offer this as an alternative to the endless circuit of guilt, fear and pity enlisted by charity publicity.

Notes

Plates

1   For reasons of space, it was not possible to include the text of the sitters which originally accompanied some of these images. The original texts and their sources can be traced via the notes. I felt it was important to credit the organisations, both disabled and non-disabled controlled, who had commissioned the work, in order to show the organisational support for new forms of disability representation.

1   Introduction

1   The word 'discourse' is to post modernism what 'bourgeois' was to modernism. It has become the 'bob-a-job' of critical theory. To make it clear, what I mean by this word is the exchange of information inside or outside a particular context at any given moment.

2   Obviously, I am alluding to Mark Rothko here. However, I think there is a case to be made on male abstract painting in particular as the mark of both chaos and control, which itself is rooted in the male existential crisis of birth and death. We are all part of the latter but only women are involved in the former.

3   On the issue of the real Shakespeare, see *The Mystery of Shakespeare* (1988) by Charlton Ogburn, London: Cardinal.

4   To witness this rise in oppressive imagery, see for example, the Disabled Photographers' Society's fellowship to a retired lecturer for his submission 'A number of the more unusual and rare medical conditions'. The retired lecturer, J. M. Trevathen Jordan, said of his work: 'Needless to say, they are not the sort of pictures most people would like on the dining room wall' (*British Journal of Photography*, 5 April 1990, p. 4). Also see the Focus for Need venture launched by the Duchess of York for the British Photographic Importers' Association. As the *British Journal of Photography* put it, 'The industry is concerned that it is losing out to a serious degree to other sectors in the competition for the consumer's purse, hence

the Focus for Need promotion' (14 March 1991). Finally, see the 1991 Photographers' Trust Fund awards. John Claridge won the Halina Award for a photograph showing a disabled person grinning, which was from a series of portraits of disabled people 'who are helped in their centres' and which was shot for the Macintyre Charity Annual Review (see *British Journal of Photography*, 21 March 1991, p. 5).

2 Social life or medical death?

1 *The Union of the Physically Impaired* (1976), quoted in *The Politics of Disablement* (1990) by Michael Oliver, London: Macmillan, pp. 3–40.

2 See, for example, *Rain Man*, with Dustin Hoffman and Tom Cruise; *My Left Foot*, with Daniel Day-Lewis; *Born on the 4th of July*, with Tom Cruise. Also see *Awakenings*, with Robert De Niro.

3 See, for example, the King's Fund Centre's 'They Are Not in the Brief', 1989. Also see the conference sequel, 'Putting Disabled People in the Brief' (the King's Fund Centre, 1989).

4 See, for example, the edited transcript of 'The BBC and Disability: A Seminar on Creating a Positive Image' (BBC, December 1990).

5 The main character in *A Gun For Sale* (1973) by Graham Greene, London: Penguin. (First published 1936.)

6 *Images of the Disabled, Disabling Images* (1987), ed. Alan Gartner and Tom Joe, New York: Praeger.

7 *Of Mice and Men* (1976) by John Steinbeck in *The Portable Steinbeck*, ed. Pascal Covice Jnr, London: Penguin.

8 *The Politics of Disablement*, op. cit., see Chapter 2.

9 ibid., p. 20.

10 ibid., p. 21.

11 ibid.

12 *Attitudes and Disabled People* (1980), ed. Victor Finkelstein, commissioned and published by the World Rehabilitation Fund, New York.

13 'A supplementary view', by Lee Meyerson and Thomas Scruggs, in *Attitudes and Disabled People*, p. 59.

14 Interview with Victor Finkelstein, 7 September 1990.

15 See for example, disabled feminists such as Jenny Morris's (1989) *Able Lives*, London: Women's Press, and *Pride Against Prejudice: Transforming Attitudes to Disability* (1991), London: Women's Press. Also see *Women with Disabilities: Essays on Psychology, Culture and Politics* (1988), ed. Michelle Fine and Adreene

Asch, Philadelphia: Temple University Press.

3   The creatures time forgot Part 1:
Into the grotto of charity advertising

1   Anonymous interview with an ex-member of the British Epilepsy Association.

2   *Charity Trends*, 13th edn (1990), Tunbridge: Charities Aid Foundation, p. 5.

3   ibid., p. 118.

4   ibid., p. 145.

5   ibid., p. 144.

6   ibid., p. 118.

7   ibid., p. 142.

8   ibid., 'Broadcast appeals: quantitative measures of success', by Diana Leat, p. 146.

9   ibid., p. 147.

10   See 'Voluntary Sector Needs – the Evidence from ITV Telethon '88' by Diana Leat, in *Charity Trends*, 12th edn (1989), Tunbridge: CAF, p. 129.

11   This was stated by a CAF Press Officer during a telephone enquiry I made to them on voluntary giving and the TV appeals. The assertion can be supported by a simple calculation of multiplying the total revenue of any particular 'Spectacular-thon' by the days in the year to find a figure less than the national daily average giving to charity!

12   *The Alms Trade: Charities Past, Present and Future* (1989) by Ian Williams, London: Unwin Hyman. Also, there is some evidence to show that the state's facilitation of individual giving through tax concessions etc. does not produce an equal rise in voluntary income. See *Sources of Charity Finance* (1989), ed. Norman Lee, Tunbridge: CAF Publications.

13   *Sources of Charity Finance* (1989), ed. Norman Lee. Quoted from the introduction by Michael Brophy, Director of the Charities Aid Foundation.

14   ibid., p. 4. Also see 'How giving creates wealth' by Barry Bracewell-Milnes, in *Charity Trends*, 13th edn (1990), p. 46.

15   The Central Statistical Office, UK accounts.

16   *The Alms Trade*, op. cit., Chapter 11.

17   Chief Commissioner Terence Fitzgerald, *Sunday Telegraph*, 24 June 1979. Quoted in *The Alms Trade*, op. cit., p. 152.

18   *The Alms Trade*, op. cit., p. 141.

19   ibid., p. 86.

20   'The most 'popular' type of charity, in

terms of both individual donations and corporate funding, remains that concerned with medicine and health' (Justin David Smith, *Charity Trends*, 12th edn, p. 7).

21 *The Alms Trade*, op.cit., p. 111.

22 ibid., p. 111.

23 *Guardian*, 28 January 1989.

24 Within the UK disability movement, one should particularly read *Disability Arts in London* for a consistent and radical rejection of the charity representation of disabled people. Also see *Link Magazine*.

25 One non-disabled attempt to question the representation, albeit on a superficial negative/positive basis, was *They Are Not in the Brief* (1989), by Susan Scott-Parker, London: the King's Fund Centre. Also, see my review of this paper in *Disability Arts in London*, no. 31, May 1989, entitled 'They are not in their briefs'.

26 Interview with Elspeth Morrison, editor of *Disability Arts in London*, 5 October 1990.

27 See *Charity Household Survey 1989/90: Who Gives What . . . and Why?* (1991), Tunbridge: CAF Publications.

28 Interview with national charity appeals director (anonymous).

29 *Charity Trends*, 13th edn, see 'Broadcast appeals: quantitative measures of success' by Diana Leat, p. 146.

30 For a notable exception to this, read Maev Kennedy's review of the same demonstration in the *Guardian*, 28 May 1990.

31 See, for example, the London Disability Arts Forum's *workhouse* cabarets.

32 Press clippings collated by Durrants Clippings Agency, London. The sample was taken from approximately 200 consumer magazines, 100 trade magazines, all the national dailies, the national Sundays, all the regional dailies, 500 weekly papers and 400 free sheets.

33 Interview with national charity head of marketing (anonymous).

34 *Charity Trends*, 13th edn (1990), Tunbridge: CAF Publications, p. 140.

35 Durrants Clippings, Jan.–March 1990.

36 'Impairment as the site of disablement.' Using the notion of the social view of disability, this criticism of charities clearly holds. However, I am aware, as I mentioned in an earlier note, of disabled feminists' views that the journey from body-as-site to society-as-site of oppression is in itself an important area of visual production. I address this in my own work in Chapter 6. Also see Jo Spence's work in Chapter 8.

37 *Daily Telegraph*, 29 August 1990.

4   The creatures time forgot Part 2:
Out of the grotto

1   See the following for examples of discussions and analysis of eugenics and disability: *Disability in the Classroom: A Civil Rights Issue* (1990), by Micheline Mason and Richard Reiser, London: ILEA. Also see 'The iron cage of visibility', by Jessica Evans, in *TEN-8 International Photography Magazine*, no. 29. Finally, I am indebted to Ruth Collett of Invalid for her talk at the 'Access to Image' Conference, National Museum of Film, Photography and Television, Bradford, 1990. Also see Chapter 9.

2   'No faith or hope in charity' by Ruth Hill in *Link Magazine*, no. 2, May 1991.

3   Interview with national charity executive member (anonymous).

4   Interview with account director of a charity-account holding ad agency (anonymous).

5   Interview with a creative director of a charity-account holding ad agency (anonymous).

6   Interview with account director of a charity-account holding ad agency (anonymous).

7   From the series of over twenty interviews with national charity and national ad agency personnel.

8   Ad agency creative director (anonymous).

9   Sources: British Epilepsy Association's published accounts for year ending 31 December 1988. Young and Rubicam's figures from Dunn and Bradstreet's *Key British Enterprises 1991*.

10   Executive member, national charity (anonymous).

11   Ad agency creative director (anonymous).

12   Ad agency account director (anonymous).

13   Ad agency account director (anonymous).

14   National charity marketing director (anonymous).

15   National charity marketing director (anonymous).

16   Ad agency account director (anonymous).

17   *Charity Trends*, 13th edn, p. 118.

18   *Charity Trends*, 12th edn, p. 100; *Charity Trends*, 13th edn, p. 118.

19   *The Charity Household Survey: Who Gives What . . . and Why?* (1991), Tunbridge: CAF Publications.

20   National charity ruling council member (anonymous).

21   National charity executive member (anonymous).

22 *Who Gives What . . . and Why?*, p. 2.

23 ibid., p. 29.

24 *Guardian*, 28 May 1991.

25 Interview with Victor Finkelstein, 7 September 1990. In particular, see his 'Disability: an administrative challenge?', in *Social Work: Disabled People and Disabling Environments*, ed. Michael Oliver (forthcoming).

5 The enfreakment of photography

1 Vic Finkelstein has argued that the 'administrative model' of disablement has replaced the 'medical model' to the extent that it is now the dominant oppressive one. This model, according to Finkelstein, suggests that the move away from the large 'phase-two' institutions (which mirrored heavy industrial production) towards the dispersal of 'care in the community' has meant that disablement has shifted from a predominantly cure-or-care issue to an administrative one. There is no doubt in my mind that this shift is being echoed in the production of 'positive' images within the UK local authorities. They are similar to the functionalist images of the charities third-stage imagery (see Chapter 4) in their portrayal of the administration of service provision to (grinning) disabled people.

2 *GYN/ecology* (1981), by Mary Daly, London: Women's Press.

3 *Images of the Disabled, Disabling Images* (1987), ed. Alan Gartner and Tom Joe, New York: Praeger.

4 *The Family of Man*, exhibition and publication by the Museum of Modern Art, New York, 1955. (Reprinted 1983.)

5 *diane arbus* (1990), London: Bloomsbury Press.

6 *On Photography* (1979), by Susan Sontag, London: Penguin.

7 'Arbus revisited: a review of the monograph', by Paul Wombell, *Portfolio* magazine, no. 10, Spring 1991.

8 ibid., p. 33.

9 *diane arbus*, op. cit., p. 23. The full title of the photograph is *Mexican Dwarf in his Hotel Room in N.Y.C. 1970*.

10 *diane arbus*, op. cit., p. 16. The full title for this photograph is: *Russian Midget Friends in a Living Room on 100th St. N.Y.C. 1963*.

11 The death cry of Kurtz on discovering the unpronounceable, in Conrad's *Heart of Darkness*.

12 *Diane Arbus: A Biography* (1984), by Patricia Bosworth, New York: Avon Books, p. 226.

13 It is important to remember that the ability of naturalist photographic prac-

tice to 'enfreak' its subject is not peculiar to the oppressive portrayal of disabled people. For example, the same process of fragmenting and reconstructing oppressed people into the projection of the photographer is particularly marked in the projection of the working classes. See *British Photography from the Thatcher Years* (book and exhibition) by Susan Kismaric, Museum of Modern Art, New York, 1990.

14   *Diane Arbus: A Biography*, op. cit., p. 227.

15   ibid., p. 153.

16   Gary Winogrand (1988), *Figments from the Real World*, ed. John Szarkowski, New York: Museum of Modern Art.

17   *The End of Art Theory: Criticism and Post-Modernity* (1986), by Victor Burgin, London: Macmillan, p. 63.

18   *Another Way of Telling* (1982), by John Berger and Jean Mohr, London: Writers and Readers.

19   ibid., p. 11.

20   For the 'left' use of disability/impairment as the site of a defence of the welfare state, see 'Bath time at St Lawrence' by Raissa Page in *TEN-8*, nos 7/8, 1982. Alternatively, for a cross-section of the inclusion of disability imagery within magazines servicing the welfare state, see the King's Fund Centre reference library, London. Finally, see the impairment charity house journals and read the photo credits, i.e. the Spastics Society's *Disability Now*. Network, Format, Report and other left photo agencies regularly supply uncritical impairment imagery.

21   *Masterpieces of Medical Photography: Selections from the Burns Archive* (1987), ed. Joel-Peter Witkin, California: Twelvetree Press.

22   *Work from a Darkroom* (1985), by Gene Lambert (exhibition and publication), Dublin: Douglas Hyde Gallery.

23   *Incurably Romantic* (1985), by Bernard F. Stehle, Philadelphia: Temple University Press.

24   *Pictures of People* (1988), by Nicholas Nixon, New York: Museum of Modern Art.

25   *Diane Arbus: A Biography* (1984), by Patricia Bosworth, New York: Avon Books, p. 365.

6   From angst into anger: the mechanics of idealism

1   *The Tempest*, by William Shakespeare, from *The Complete Works of William Shakespeare* (1979), ed. Peter Alexander, London: Collins.

2   See, for example, *Management Today*, London: IPC Magazines.

3   Apart from charity advertising, see most voluntary sector annual reports, trade union journals, left photo agencies from Magnum to Network, and so on for images of victims photographed and contexted not by themselves but by their (often self-appointed) 'advocates'.

4   The National Union of Journalists' *Freelance Rates Guide 89* recommends rates for provincial newspapers at as low as £35 per half-day. (One must bear in mind that half of this fee is likely to be spent on the general upkeep and purchase of the photographer's tools.)

5   A Sense of Self (1988), touring exhibition and catalogue. Available from Camerawork Gallery, 121 Roman Rd, London E2 OQN, tel: 081 980 6256.

6   Much of my understanding of a theory of the *subject* in radical photography has come from numerous discussions with Jo Spence. Thanks Jo.

7   Striking Poses: a 30-panel (15 b/w, 15 colour) touring exhibition with text and a poster and card, is available either from the Graeae Theatre Co., London, on 071 383 7492 (minicom)/071 383 7541 or from Camerawork.

8   For an analysis of the notion of the beginning of patriarchy and the split of the self into mind/body, feeling/seeing, reality/representation, see the works of Robert Graves, particularly *The Greek Myths*, Vols I and II, or *The White Goddess*. For a feminist exploration and analysis of the roots and meaning of patriarchy, see Mary Daly's (1981) *GYN/ecology*, London: Women's Press.

9   For the text to the five images used (written by the sitters), see the Beyond the Barriers exhibition and catalogue: Camerawork, 121 Roman Rd, London E2 OQN (tel: 081 980 6256).

10   See Chapter 7, 'Revolt of the species! A theory of the subject'.

11   For examples of the images as reportage illustrations see *Irish Post*, 16 February 1991; *Irish in Britain News*, 15 February 1991; *Republican News*, 21 February 1991.

12   For an illustration of how this worked, See 'Image Makers: Eamonn McCabe on Dave Hevey's compassionate eye', *Guardian*, Saturday/Sunday, 23/24 February 1991.

13   See *Disability Arts in London*; the singers Johnny Crescendo and Ian Stanton; comedians such as Allan Sutherland; compères such as Natalie Markham and Elspeth Morrison; members of The Tragic but Brave Roadshow; and so on for examples of acid and anarchic 'crip' humour.

7   Revolt of the species! A theory of the subject

1   *On Photography* (1978), by Susan Sontag, London: Penguin.

2 *Camera Lucida: Reflections on Photography* (1984), by Roland Barthes, trans. Richard Howard, London: Fontana.

3 *Thinking Photography* (1982), ed. Victor Burgin, London: Macmillan.

4 *The End of Art Theory: Criticism and Postmodernity* (1986), by Victor Burgin, London: Macmillan.

5 *Photography/Politics One* (1979), ed. by Terry Dennett, David Evans, Sylvia Gohl and Jo Spence, London: Photography Workshop. *Photography/Politics Two* (1986), ed. by Patricia Holland, Jo Spence and Simon Watney, London: Methuen/Photography Workshop.

6 *Putting Myself in the Picture* (1986), by Jo Spence, London: Camden Press.

7 *Photography Against the Grain: Essays and Photo Works 1973–1983* (1984), by Allan Sekula, Press of the Novia Scotia College of Art and Design.

8 *Decoding Advertisements: Ideology and Meaning in Advertising* (1978), by Judith Williamson, London and New York: Marion Boyars.

9 *The End of Art Theory*, op. cit., p. 64.

10 ibid., p. 198.

11 *Photography Against the Grain*, op. cit., Preface xi.

12 Quoted by Jo Spence and Rosie Martin. 'Photo-therapy: psychic realism as a healing art?', *TEN-8*, no. 30, Autumn 1988, p. 2.

13 Camerawork Gallery also organised the disabled-only conference, 'Cap in Hand', February (1991) in response to the King's Fund Centre Conference.

14 The ad hoc group's eight-point demands to the King's Fund Centre, drafted by David Hevey.

15 'A code of ethics for disability imagery in the media' (provisional title), by Colin Barnes, London: British Council of Organisations of Disabled People, to be published in 1992.

16 'The bargain' (1988), by Mary Johnson in *The Disability Rag*, September/October, pp. 5–8.

17 ibid., p. 6.

18 *FDR's Splendid Deception* (1985), by Hugh G. Gallagher, New York: Dodd Mead & Co.

19 A glossary of some of the organisations which have given substantial economic support for the entire Creatures project (which includes this book, a national poster series, a touring exhibition, a training pack and a seminar – see Camerawork for full details on 081 980 6256) includes the Arts Council of Great Britain, the Greater London Arts, Camerawork Gallery (London), the Rowntree Foundation (UK), etc. All of them are non-disabled controlled.

20 *Camera Lucida: Reflections on Photography* (1984), by Roland Barthes, trans. Richard Howard, London: Fontana Paperbacks, p. 31.

21 The recent prices paid for Van Gogh's *Sunflowers* may show that painting is far from dead (although it might be argued that the valuation and fetishism of oil painting's Once Only-ness is essentially necrophiliac, since the uniqueness of any particular body of work is only complete after the physical death of the artist).

22 *Camera Lucida*, op. cit, p. 88.

23 *The End of Art Theory*, op. cit., p. 88.

24 See Chapter 7.

25 Quoted in *The Audience As Actor and Character* (1989), by Sidney Williams, London and Toronto: Bucknell University Press, p. 35.

26 *Theatre of the Oppressed* (1989), by Augusto Boal, London: Pluto Press.

27 ibid., Chapter 1.

28 ibid., p. 34.

29 ibid.

30 ibid.

31 *William Shakespeare: The Complete Works* (1979), ed. Peter Alexander, London and Glasgow: Collins, p. 701.

32 *The Theatre of Bertolt Brecht* (1986), by John Willett, London: Methuen.

33 ibid., p. 170.

34 ibid., p. 172.

35 *Absurd Drama* (1965), Intro. by Martin Esslin, London: Penguin.

36 *American Alternative Theatre* (1988), by Theodore Shank, London: Macmillan.

37 *The Theatre of Images* (1977), ed. Bonnie Marrance, New York: PAJ Publications.

38 *Theatre of the Oppressed*, op. cit., p. 46.

39 Jo Spence. Conversations with the author, May/June 1991. Also see *Family Snaps: The Meanings of Domestic Photography* (1991), ed. by Jo Spence and Patricia Holland, London: Virago Press.

40 Of course, graphics and other design considerations can alter the meaning after the optics. However, where this is the case, the image will have been shot to suit the grid into which it is intended to orbit.

41 By no means am I suggesting that this workshop process is at all exhaustive. However, it is a process which I have worked on with a number of disabled workers ranging from equality trainers to theatre and photograph workers as well as the disabled people who have attended my workshops. I am also aware that other disabled photographers, like Jo Spence, deliberately use the void in image-making. For example, her phototherapy work would not use

Polaroids because the drama of the exposure of feelings might be interrupted. In other words, trust in representation in a workshop space can be established by any number of methods. See 'Remodelling photo history, 1981–82' (1986), pp. 118–33.

42   For a general guide to physically accessing photography, see *Eliminating Shadows: A Manual on Photography and Disability* (1990), by Ray Cooper and Ronald Cooper, London: London Print Workshop.

43   Although physical access into photographic equipment and organisations is far from total, the conditions exist (technically at least) whereby access is enforceable through the disability movement and other political pressures. See *Photography and Disability in England* (1990), by Ad Lib, London: Arts Council.

9   Towards a disability imagery currency
Part 2: *Little Stephen*

1   See *The Politics of Mental Handicap* (1980), by Johanna Ryan and Frank Thomas, London: Pelican.

2   For instance, Professor Illingworth, one of the most widely known paediatricians said, of Down's Syndrome, for the most part incorrectly, in his manual for teachers in 1974:

after about seven years they develop a fissured tongue, and later years about 10 per cent develop cataracts. Puberty is delayed, and most are infertile. Mongols are all retarded in development their mean IQ is 28 . . . They hardly ever learn to read or write – or at least to read or write with understanding. They are all retarded in development their development slows down after the first six to nine months. There is a common statement, repeated from textbook to textbook, that mongols are placid, easy to manage and musical. This is incorrect. Many studies have shown that they are no different in behaviour from other equally defective children, and they are not musical. Half die by the age of 5. They are prone to respiratory tract infections. They tend to become fat because of relative inactivity.
(Open University Special Needs in Education E241/Unit 13, p. 28)

3   See M. Foucault (1984), 'The politics of health in the eighteenth century', in *The Foucault Reader*, ed. Paul Rabinow, Harmondsworth: Penguin.

4   On eugenics, see David Green's 'Veins of resemblance' in the *Oxford Art Journal*, vol. 7, no. 2, 1984. The supposed link between degeneracy and racial ranking has left us with one

legacy. The designation of 'mongolian idiocy' or mongolism for the chromosonal disorder of Tri-21 was first classified by Dr Langdon Down in the 1860s. Dr Down likened idiocy with the working classes and was worried about the propagation of an enfeebled race. Recording visual similarities of eyes and skin colour of mongolian nationals with some 'idiots', his perceptions fitted the nineteenth-century theory of recapitulation which held that certain forms of 'idiocy' were arrested development from an earlier phase in the white male evolution. Dr Down's eurocentric views led him to view certain 'idiots' as mongols. Dr Down said, 'The boy's aspect is such that it is difficult to realise that he is the child of Europeans but so fre-quently are these characteristics (thick lips, wrinkled foreheads, sparse hair) presented, that there can be no doubt that these ethnic features are the result of degeneration.' Quoted in S.J. Gould (1981), *The Mismeasure of Man*, London: Pelican. See also the essay on Dr Down in *The Panda's Thumb* (1980), by S.J. Gould, London: Pelican.

5 See pamphlet, 'Helping to live or allowing to die?' by the Campaign for Mental Handicaps, 1981; also see Ann Shearer, 'Everybody's ethics: what future for handicapped babies?', CMH, 1984.

6 Sekula in 'Dismantling modernism, reinventing documentary' in *Photography/Politics One*, London: Photography Workshop (1980), p. 173.

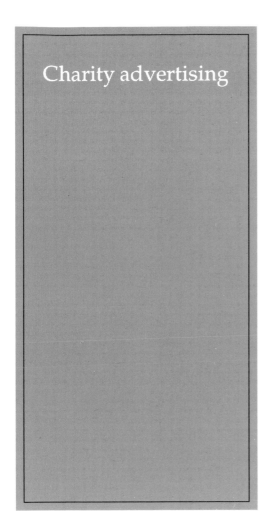
Charity advertising

1 Spastics Society poster:
   Could this be where I got my Spirit of
   Adventure and my Love for Camping?

2 Spastics Society poster:
   Everyone Assumes I Won't Want to
   Get to the Top.

3 The Multiple Sclerosis Society poster:
   How Does it Feel to Have a Mental
   Age of Thirty and a Physical Age of
   One?

4 Spastics Society poster:
   Just Because I Couldn't Speak, They
   Thought I had Nothing to Say.

5 Mencap poster:
   A Mental Handicap is There for Life.
   So is Mencap.

Plate 1

Could this be where I got my spirit of adventure and my love for camping?

The only reason I've got cerebral palsy is that I couldn't breathe when I was born.

A week in an oxygen tent could not prevent the fact that every time my brain tells my body to do something, my body makes like a demented octopus.

But it's only a disability (yes, only), something The Spastics Society understands.

So much so that when I went to two of the Society's special schools, by far the most important thing I learned was how to stick up for myself and to organise life the way I want it.

They positively encouraged independence. And the time you really feel you have won is when you forget the Society is there at all.

Like when you're camping, which I do regularly. In fact, I'll never forget the time I once rolled out of my tent, accidentally and at three in the morning.

The moon was shining and everything was still, except for the odd high speed train that whistled past my ear on the main Exeter to London line.

My childlike instinct was to call out for help. Luckily nobody heard.

So I told myself not to be so stupid and for once my body responded.

I crawled and crawled up the hill till I got back to the tent.

Because there's nothing like doing it yourself. Is there?

FOR HELP INFORMATION OR TO MAKE A DONATION WRITE TO THE SPASTICS SOCIETY AT 12 PARK CRESCENT, LONDON W1N 4EQ. TEL: (01) 636 5020.
NAME
ADDRESS   POSTCODE
AMOUNT £   FOR ACCESS OR VISA DONATIONS PLEASE STATE CARD NO.   SIGNATURE

THE SPASTICS SOCIETY
FOR PEOPLE WITH CEREBRAL PALSY

Opening minds by opening doors.

Plate 2

"Everyone assumes I won't want to get to the top."

Our biggest handicap is other people's attitude.
THE SPASTICS SOCIETY

Plate 3

How

does it feel to have

a mental age of

thirty and a physical

age of one?

Plate 4

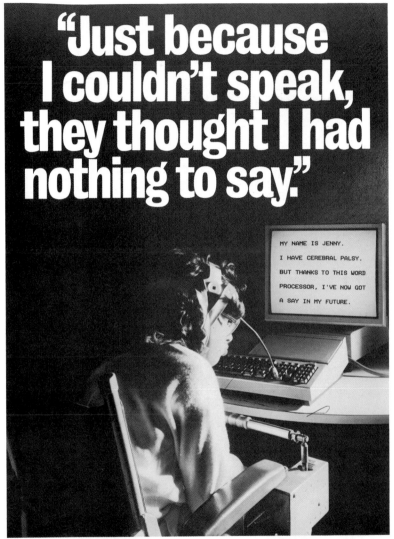

Plate 5

From the touring
exhibition
Striking Poses,
commissioned by the
Graeae Theatre
Company

Plate 6

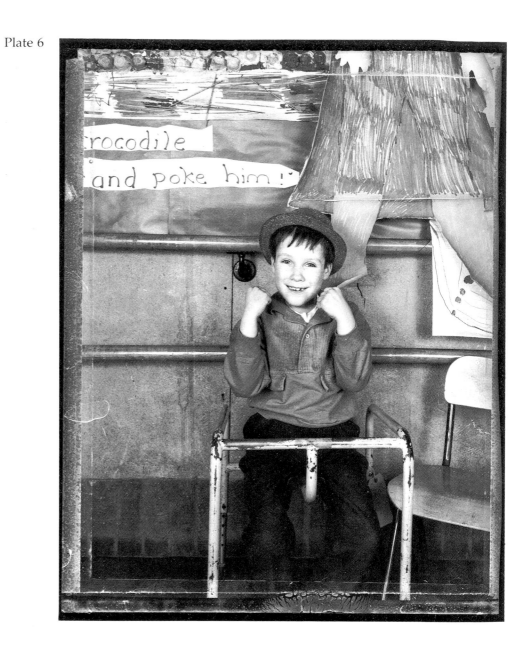

Plate 7

Plate 8

Plate 9

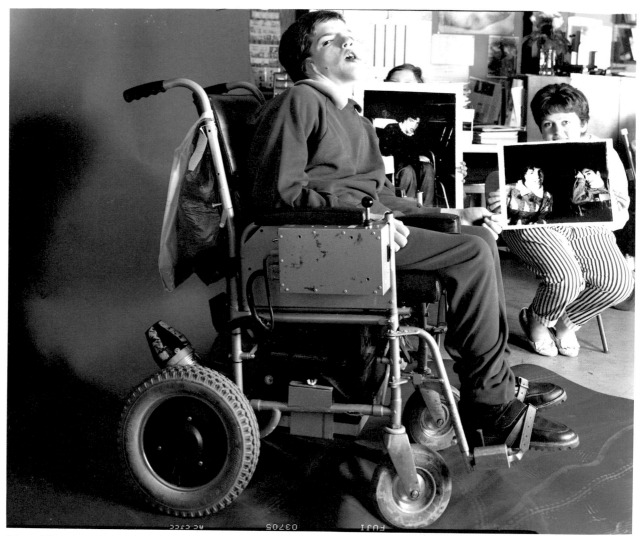

Plate 10

Plate 11

Plate 12

Plate 13

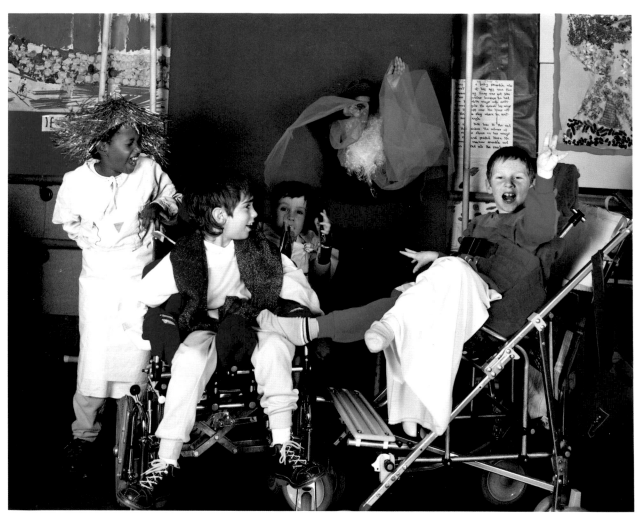

Plate 14

From the touring
exhibition
A Sense of Self,
commissioned by
Camerawork Gallery,
London

15   Phillipa, Weaver

16   Derek (RIP), from the Effra Trust

17   Ian, from the Effra Trust

18   Anonymous: Epilepsy. 'Either the well
     was deep or she fell very slowly' (Lewis
     Carroll, Alice in Wonderland)

Plate 15

Plate 16

Plate 17

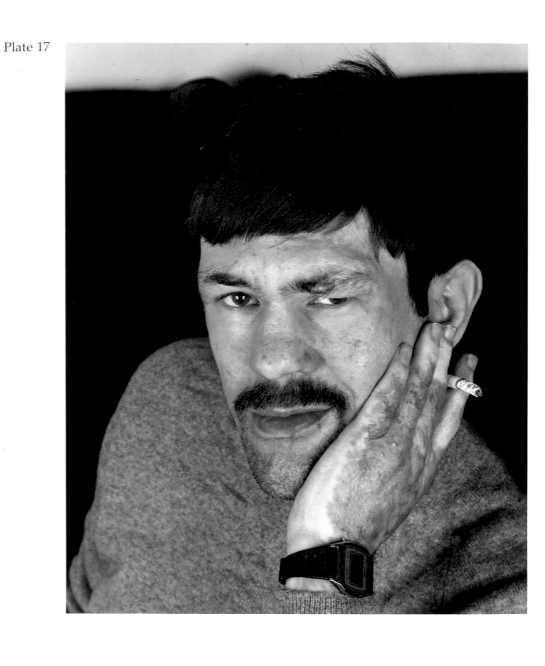

Plate 18

From the touring exhibition Beyond the Barriers

Disability, Sexuality and Personal Relationships, commissioned by Camerawork Gallery

Plate 19

Plate 20

Plate 21

Plate 22

Plate 23

Plate 24

Work commissioned by local authorities, voluntary organisations and trade unions

25   Liberty, Equality, Disability
       One image from a series of five posters commissioned by Southwark local authority

26   Theirs by Right
       One image from a series of five posters and a touring exhibition commissioned by Camden local authority

27   CSV Annual Report
       One image from shoots for the annual report of the Community Service Volunteers' Agency

28   Access is not Enough
       Cover of the National Union of Civil and Public Servants (NUCPS) and one image from a touring exhibition of the same name, commissioned by the NUCPS

29   Summer in the City
       One image of two deaf boys from a touring exhibition commissioned by Hammersmith local authority

Plate 25

Plate 26

Plate 27

Plate 28

June 1990 Volume 3 Number 6
Published by the National Union of Civil and Public Servants.
ISSN 0957 8978.

the National Union

JOURNAL

Inside

Yes to 8.5 per cent!
Yes to merger
with the CPSA!

Full conference reports

Access is not enough
Disabled in the Civil Service

Plate 29

The Creatures Time Forgot

PART 1:

The Process of Disablement from the Camerawork touring exhibition The Creatures Time Forgot: Photography and the Construction of Disability Imagery

Plate 30

Plate 31

Plate 32

Plate 33

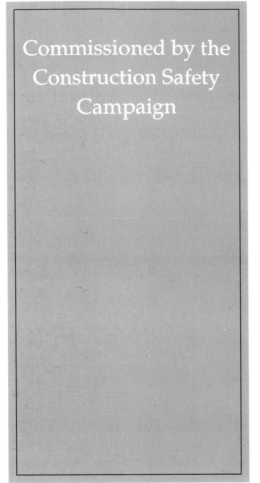

Commissioned by the
Construction Safety
Campaign

Plate 34

Plate 35

Plate 36

The Creatures Time Forgot

PART 2:

Liberty, Equality, Disability –
Images from a Movement.
Distributed by Camerawork,
and part of the
Camerawork touring exhibition
The Creatures Time Forgot:
Photography and the Construction
of Disability Imagery. Funded by
the Rowntree Foundation

Plate 37

LIBERTY EQUALITY DISABILITY

These posters are part of **The Creatures Time Forgot: Photography & The Construction of Disability Imagery** by David Hevey, in association with Camerawork Gallery. This project also includes a publication (Routledge), a touring exhibition and training pack (Camerawork 081-980 6256). These posters are **free** and are distributed by Camerawork, London. *Number one of seven.*

SUPPORTED BY JR JOSEPH ROWNTREE FOUNDATION

PRODUCED AND PHOTOGRAPHED BY DAVID HEVEY. FUNDED BY THE JOSEPH ROWNTREE FOUNDATION

"I've always been angry. It's only when I met other disabled people that I realised I wasn't alone in this. Most of my childhood was shaped by the hospital. The scars from the hip surgery are the railroad tracks of somebody else's journey and the effects of institutionalisation are hard to live with. Politically, my fluctuating impairment and I are comfortable. The disability, those years of not owning my body, still cause anger but now it's becoming constructive; it is society that is wrong, not me."

IMAGES OF A MOVEMENT

Designed by Clive Wilson 071-603 6272 Printed by Originals Plus

Plate 38

Plate 39

LIBERTY EQUALITY DISABILITY

These posters are part of
**The Creatures Time Forgot: Photography
& The Construction of Disability Imagery**
by David Hevey, in association with
Camerawork Gallery. This project also
includes a publication (Routledge), a
touring exhibition and training pack
(Camerawork 081-980 6256). These
posters are **free** and are distributed by
Camerawork, London.
Number three of seven.

"I resent the idea of
operations to save my
hearing. I went along
with them in the past
because I didn't know
myself as a deaf person.
I had experienced racism
always, but as an actor I
was shocked by the
discrimination against
me as a deaf person.
Eventually, you stop
trying to fool yourself and
you respect what you are.
You spend your life
finding your black
culture, your pride, then
you find, actually, there's
a deaf culture. This gives
you a language - you are
black, deaf and
articulate."
Ray

IMAGES
OF A
MOVEMENT

Plate 40

LIBERTY EQUALITY DISABILITY

These posters are part of **The Creatures Time Forgot: Photography & The Construction of Disability Imagery** by David Hevey, in association with Camerawork Gallery. This project also includes a publication (Routledge), a touring exhibition and training pack (Camerawork 081-980 6256). These posters are **free** and are distributed by Camerawork, London.
Number four of seven

PRODUCED AND PHOTOGRAPHED BY DAVID HEVEY.   FUNDED BY THE JOSEPH ROWNTREE FOUNDATION.

"In the end it is only relationships which matter or which give our lives meaning. This is why I believe a 'special' segregated education system is so harmful to society, because it depends for its existence on the breaking of relationships. An inclusive education system will have to rate friendship at least as highly as spelling. Then, we will be appalled at how little we know or understand about each other."
Micheline

IMAGES OF A MOVEMENT

Designed by Clive Wilson 071 603 6272 Printed by Originals Plus

Plate 41

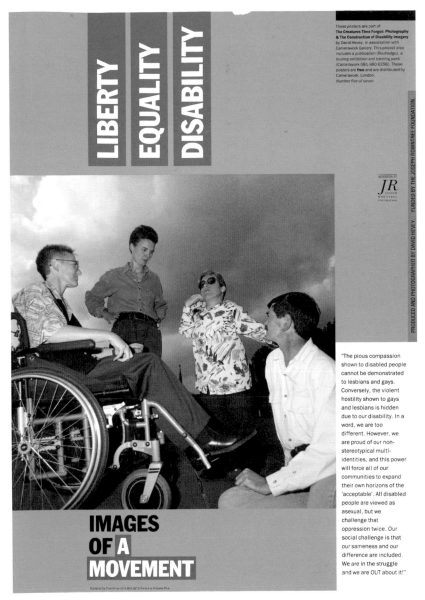

LIBERTY EQUALITY DISABILITY

IMAGES OF A MOVEMENT

These posters are part of **The Creatures Time Forgot: Photography & The Construction of Disability Imagery** by David Hevey, in association with Camerawork Gallery. This project also includes a publication (Routledge), a touring exhibition and training pack (Camerawork 081-980 6256). These posters are **free** and are distributed by Camerawork, London.
Number five of seven

PRODUCED AND PHOTOGRAPHED BY DAVID HEVEY.   FUNDED BY THE JOSEPH ROWNTREE FOUNDATION.

"The pious compassion shown to disabled people cannot be demonstrated to lesbians and gays. Conversely, the violent hostility shown to gays and lesbians is hidden due to our disability. In a word, we are too different. However, we are proud of our non-stereotypical multi-identities, and this power will force all of our communities to expand their own horizons of the 'acceptable'. All disabled people are viewed as asexual, but we challenge that oppression twice. Our social challenge is that our sameness and our difference are included. We are in the struggle and we are OUT about it!"

Plate 42

LIBERTY
EQUALITY
DISABILITY

Altrincham 41

IMAGES
OF A
MOVEMENT

These posters are part of
**The Creatures Time Forgot: Photography
& The Construction of Disability Imagery**
by David Hevey, in association with
Camerawork Gallery. This project also
includes a publication (Routledge), a
touring exhibition and training pack
(Camerawork 081-980 6256). These
posters are **free** and are distributed by
Camerawork, London.
Number six of seven

SUPPORTED BY
JR
JOSEPH
ROWNTREE
FOUNDATION

PRODUCED AND PHOTOGRAPHED BY DAVID HEVEY. FUNDED BY THE JOSEPH ROWNTREE FOUNDATION.

"It is not our impairments
or 'medical conditions'
that determine our
quality of life. It is the
negative planning, the
non-consultation,
segregation in education
and inaccessible
architecture which create
disability. Workplaces
rarely admit us,
employers discriminate
against us and services
are planned so that we
cannot use them.
Wherever there is
inaccessible transport or
inaccessible buildings or
inaccessible
information, there will be
disabled people. It is
plain and simple:
Access, Rights,
Emancipation!"

Designed by Clive Wilson 071-603 6272 Printed by Originals Plus

The Creatures Time Forgot

PART 3:

In the Charity Camp.
From the
Camerawork touring exhibition
The Creatures Time Forgot:
Photography and the Construction
of Disability Imagery

CAP IN HAND

Plate 43

THANK YOU

FOR PUTTING US IN COLOUR

Plate 44

IF THE CAP FITS

GIVE IT AN ANTI-CONVULSANT

Plate 45

Commissions by the
London Disability
Arts Forum, the Save
the Children Fund,
the Inner London
Education
Association

Plate 46

Plate 47

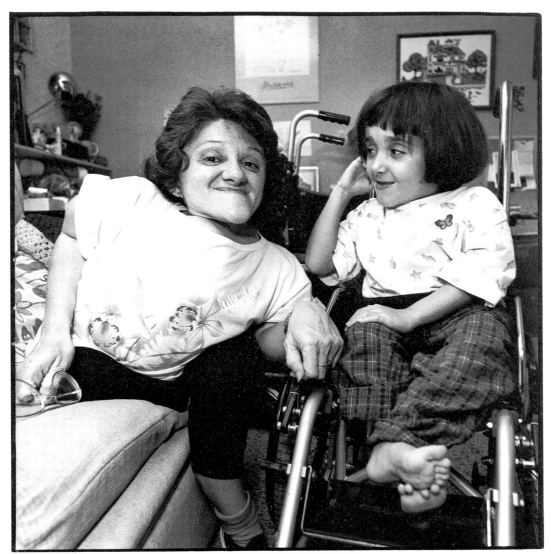

Plate 48

Plate 49

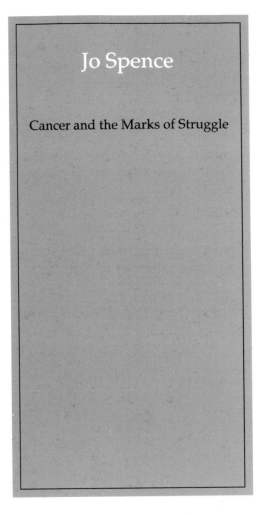

Jo Spence

Cancer and the Marks of Struggle

Plate 50

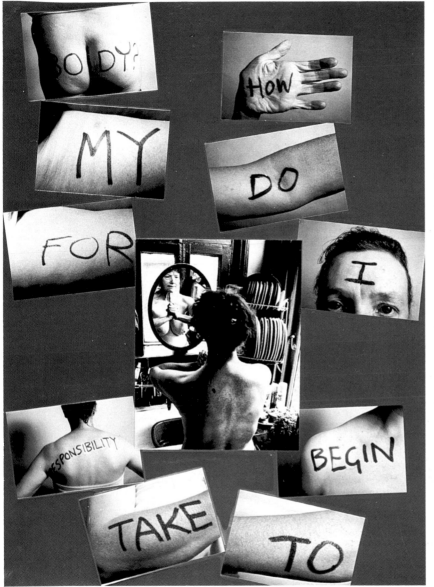

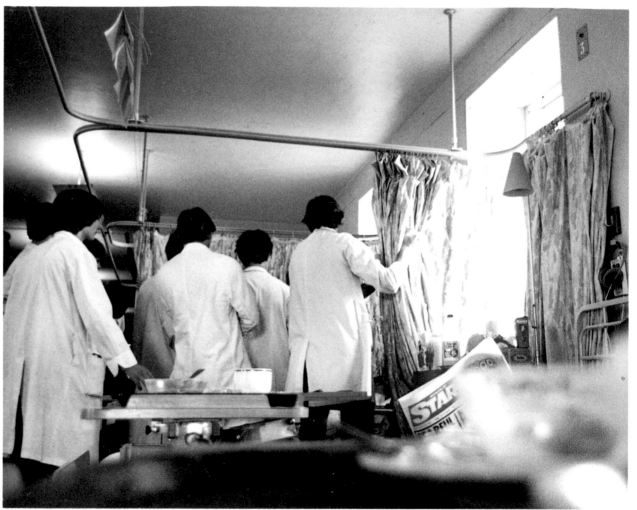

Plate 51

Plate 52

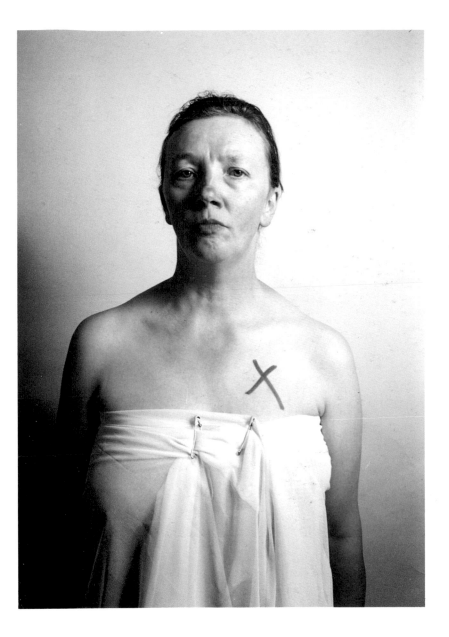

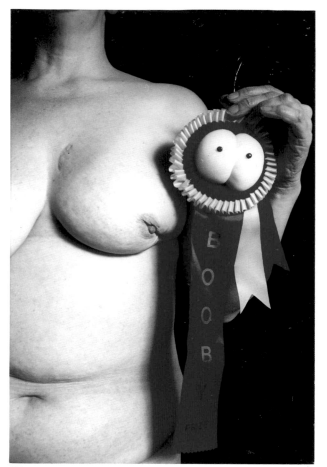

Plate 53

Plate 54

Jessica Evans and Andy Golding

From their series
Hidden Menace:
See how the Charity Agents
Caught the Defectives
who Roam our Streets

Plate 55

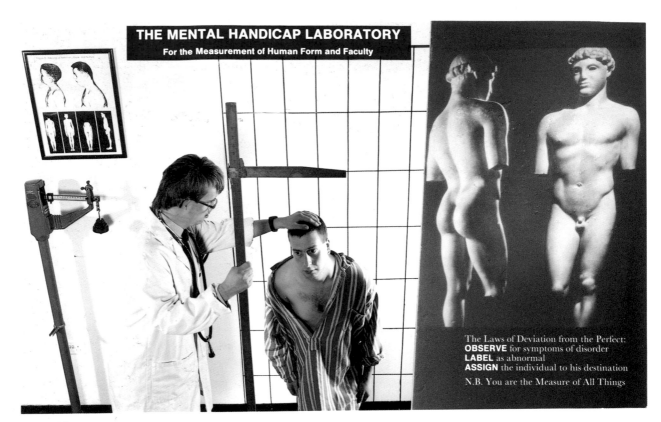

Plate 56

THEY SAID IT COULDN'T HAPPEN HERE!

(We are)
categorised by you
segregated in 'special schools'
denied job opportunities
sterilised without consent
drugged to keep us quiet
ignored when we speak
represented as monsters

Freedom? Equality? Democracy?

Plate 57

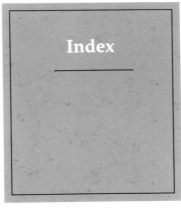

Index